The Vacant Chair

Paul Schnitzler. *"He Returns No More."* 1868. Ink and watercolor.
*(Collection of Whitney Museum of American Art. Gift of Edgar William
and Bernice Chrysler Garbisch)*

THE
VACANT
CHAIR

*The Northern Soldier
Leaves Home*

REID MITCHELL

New York   Oxford
OXFORD UNIVERSITY PRESS
1993

Oxford University Press

Oxford   New York   Toronto
Delhi   Bombay   Calcutta   Madras   Karachi
Kuala Lumpur   Singapore   Hong Kong   Tokyo
Nairobi   Dar es Salaam   Cape Town
Melbourne   Auckland   Madrid

and associated companies in
Berlin   Ibadan

Copyright © 1993 by Reid Mitchell

Published by Oxford University Press, Inc.,
200 Madison Avenue, New York, New York 10016

Oxford is a registered trademark of Oxford University Press

Library of Congress Cataloging-in-Publication Data
Mitchell, Reid.
The vacant chair : the Northern soldier leaves home /
Reid Mitchell.
p.   cm.
Includes bibliographical references and index.
ISBN 0–19–507893–4
1. United States—History—Civil War, 1861–1865—Social aspects.
2. United States. Army—History—Civil War, 1861–1865.
3. United States. Army—Military life—History—19th century.
I. Title.   E468.9.M68   1993
973.7'1—dc20   92–36921

The second epigraph is taken from Melissa Green, *The Squanicook Eclogues* (New York:
W. W. Norton and Company, 1987.) I thank W. W. Norton for allowing me to quote these lines.
An earlier version of chapter two first appeared as "The Northern Society and His Community," in
Maris A. Vinovskis, editor, *Toward a Social History of the American Civil War* (New York:
Cambridge University Press, 1990). Grateful acknowledgment is made to Cambridge University
Press for permission to use this material.

2 4 6 8 9 7 5 3 1

Printed in the United States of America
on acid-free paper

for
Virginia Louise Adams Mitchell
and
Elisabeth Anne Buurma

Acknowledgments

Three of these chapters have been published in earlier form. The first written—Chapter Two—was published in Maris Vinovskis, ed., *Towards a Social History of the American Civil War* (New York: Cambridge University Press, 1990). The second written—now Chapter One—was published in Catherine Clinton and Nina Silber, eds., *Divided Houses* (New York: Oxford University Press, 1992). A much different version of the Afterword appeared in Gabor Boritt, ed., *Why the Confederacy Lost* (New York: Oxford University Press, 1992). Writing for these three collections helped me conceive of *The Vacant Chair*. I owe particular thanks to two of the editors: Clinton literally pulled me off a barstool in New Orleans during a meeting of the Southern Historical Association and demanded I write an essay on the Civil War as a coming-of-age experience; and Boritt telephoned me to ask if there was any way to apply my work on the social history of the soldier to the problem of Confederate defeat and Union victory.

Several colleagues at Princeton University helped me. In particular, Christine Stansell commented on two chapters of this book while it was in draft. Judith Hunter shared her work-in-progress with me, helped me with bibliography, and commented on the entire manuscript. At Oxford University Press, Sheldon Meyer's enthusiasm for the project cheered me.

Long before I was sure I would write this book, Liza Buurma was its strongest advocate. She read the book in draft, made useful suggestions, and insisted on retaining the subtitle. She has also made it ever more necessary for me to try to understand northerners. Thanks.

Metuchen, N.J.   Reid Mitchell
March 1993

Contents

Introduction
"Other Mothers' Boys":
Domestic Imagery and the
Northern Soldier

John J. Ryder remembered growing up in an ideal home.
That was the doing of Mercy Jenkins Ryder, his mother.
Ryder's father had died, leaving his widow two children to
rear. "It was a heart-breaking loss to us all, especially to
Mother, but she always had an unwavering faith in God as a
Heavenly Father upon whose guidance she implicitly relied."
Mercy Ryder raised her boys in prayer and kindness, with
morning Bible readings.

When Abraham Lincoln called for troops in 1861, Mercy
Ryder forbade John's enlistment. While he waited for her permission, the Cape Cod boy joined a temporary company which
drilled to fife and drum and fired blanks. "One-third wore red
shirts, one-third white, and one-third blue—no coats or vests."
This colorful group was commanded by officers dressed in
Revolutionary War uniforms. It lasted until fishing season.

In 1862, John Ryder was on a fishing voyage when the news arrived that his hometown had a quota of five men to supply the Union army. He went home to enlist. That day, however, Mercy Ryder fell ill. "She was never strong, and the thought of my leaving home for the uncertainties of a soldier's life so affected her heart that she could only say, 'Oh, John, say you won't go, or I shall die.'" Ryder agreed to stay but the next morning Mercy Ryder had changed her mind. She had prayed during the night, and learned her duty. "I knew other mothers' boys must go, and now you have my consent and blessing."[1]

In her own way—and with some reluctance—Mercy Ryder proved a good Republican Mother. John Ryder met what northerners regarded as the most reliable test of a young man's loyalty; he volunteered to put down the rebellion. Linda K. Kerber has shown that the figure of the Republican Mother was created following the Revolution as part of the development of "an ideology for women's education in a republic, defending improvement in education without repudiating the relationship of women to their households." A Republican Mother raised virtuous Republican Children. Her boys became the men that the Republic would draw upon for leadership. Kerber explains that "The influence women had on children, especially sons, gave them ultimate responsibility for the future of the new nation." The task of the Republican Mother required education which custom had denied to women—but the focus of her education was her family. "A woman's competence was not assumed to extend to the making of political decisions. Her political task was accomplished within the confines of her family."[2]

Yet in Ryder's account of his mother, much of the content of Republican Motherhood has been drained. Original advocates of Republican Motherhood justified education for women as a way that they could better instill patriotic virtue within their sons. But later emphasis on women's superior morality made education for motherhood seem almost superfluous—of course, only after common school reform had made education for girls almost ubiquitous in the North. Mercy Ryder succeeded in making her son John patriotic, but she did so with kindness, devotion, and the Bible. Her character, not her intellect, was the key to her fulfilling her role as an American mother.[3]

I do not claim that John Ryder's memories of Mercy Jenkins Ryder explain that woman particularly well. Ryder's image of his mother concerns us here. Years after his enlistment, years after her death, he presented his mother as the most important influence in his life, including his decision to serve in the Union army. His published memoirs even open with a photograph of his mother. To his mind, the link between her virtue and piety and his service was direct. She had made him into the kind of boy that wished to fight for the Union even though that desire pained her. Ryder shared his vision of an innately virtuous mother who inculcated patriotism with many of the other men of the Civil War era. The popular song "Can I Go Dearest Mother!" portrayed "the flame of ardor on a loyal mother's part" and a son who told her "To be faithful to my country I have ever learned from you."[4]

This book is about the John Ryders of the Civil War, not the Mercy Ryders. It is not a book about domesticity. It is a book about how what we might call "domestic imagery"—images of home and the family—shaped the ways in which northern soldiers experienced the Civil War. When these men spoke of the Union as a family, it was less than an identity, but it was more than a metaphor. The centrality of home and the family to northern culture made them central to the northern soldier's understanding of the Civil War. This was a culture in which, according to one popular song, just before going into battle, the soldier considers not the issues that have led his country to this war, nor death, God, and his ultimate fate, but his mother—"just before the battle, mother, I am thinking most of you."[5]

This is a book about John Ryder and those whom Mercy Ryder called "other mothers' boys." This book, therefore, represents an attempt to put together two different historical literatures—that which deals with gender studies, domesticity, and the family, and that which deals with the Civil War. It also represents—after that historiographic synthesis has been piously wished for—a personal search for a way to integrate the visions of the northern soldier as a man at war, the northern soldier as a citizen, and the northern soldier as a human possessed of intimate relations.[6]

The reference—or the image—I have chosen to represent this domestic ideology during the war is "the vacant chair." "The Vacant Chair," of course, was the title of a sentimental song, a Civil War tearjerker by George Frederick Root. "We shall meet, but we shall miss him," sing those whom the now-dead soldier left at home, "There will be one vacant chair." Although in the song, the family's soldier is gone for ever, only to be remembered in their nightly prayers, "The Vacant Chair" would have resonance in northern households whether or not the soldiers they had sent to the war were living or dead. Soldiering leaves the chair vacant; death while soldiering leaves it more vacant still. At the same time—and the song deliberately makes this painful—the family's life continues, must continue, without him. But the chair remains, to symbolize the soldier's absence. It would not do to put the chair away; it must be left for him, claiming the place that he perhaps one day shall reclaim. The vacant chair holds the soldier's place at the family table for him. It represents his ultimate return to the family and home that give meaning to his absence itself.

The Vacant Chair

We shall meet but we shall miss him
There will be one vacant chair
George Frederick Root
"The Vacant Chair"

I haven't come to rob but reconcile
the way the dead were wounded with my blood.
What does a private history conceal?
And will it tell me why the decades bled?

. . .

That child who cupped her chin and dreamt is dust.
Tongues and tribes have multiplied and died.
Ten thousand revolutions, unredressed,
have turned the sun's eye bloody, yet our dead
still write to us, and we are torn by what we read.
Melissa Green
"New Year's Day 1986"
The Attic Bird

1

Soldiering, Manhood, and Coming of Age

WHEN Abraham Lincoln first ran for president, Cyrus F. Boyd was already twenty-four years old. Nevertheless he would later say that he and the other Republican boys of Palmyra, Iowa, "organized a company of young men just young enough and strong enough to do some tall yelling." They must have been a sight—each one wearing blue overalls, white shirts, and "a chip hat," riding horseback to electioneer for Lincoln. "We were supposed to be assisting Abraham Lincoln to be elected President and everybody now knows that he was elected." The horses, he later confessed, were really colts. "We not only had to break and drill ourselves but had to break the *colts* also and at the same time."

This frolicking lot of young politicians became one of the companies Iowa contributed to the Union war effort. "When our man Lincoln called for men to suppress the insurrection we did not respond the first time but at the next call we left the colts at home and went almost to [a] *boy*." The word "boy" and indeed the emphasis are not mine but Boyd's himself, when he looked back years later at the events of the Civil War. Later in

3

life, Boyd took his wartime diary and rewrote it into an account of his months in the Fifteenth Iowa Infantry Regiment,
the regiment in which he served until he left to become an
officer in another outfit. This autobiography, a mixture of a
young man's diary and an old man's reflections, he sent to a
friend of his who had soldiered with him in the Fifteenth Iowa.
Cyrus F. Boyd self-consciously molded his autobiographical
tale of service in the army into a story about a boy becoming a
man—making soldiering a coming-of-age experience. He obviously expected his friend would recognize this story and
share this understanding of their youthful joint service in the
Union army.[1]

This vision, this credo of masculinity, maturation, and
military service, was hardly unique to Cyrus F. Boyd or to the
Civil War. Both during the years 1861 through 1865 and all
through the postwar period, as Americans tried to make sense
of their war, they linked the transformation of the civilian into
a soldier and the passage of a boy into adulthood. At the mini-
mum, the relationship was twofold. First, with a great number
of American youth—defined roughly as those still living
within a parental household—joining the army, those who
lived through the war arrived at the age traditionally associated with full manhood. They "came of age" during the war
and the war had to be part of that experience. Second, the very
ideas of man, soldier, and citizen were inextricably linked.
Remaining a civilian was thought unmanly; going to war a
proof of manhood. Since coming of age means not simply becoming an adult but assuming adult gender roles—becoming a
man—popular thought sometimes conflated the two transfor-
mations. And so did many of the young men who served in the
armies.[2]

Considering the age of many Union soldiers, as well as
their Confederate counterparts, the stress on war as a maturing
process is hardly surprising. Gerald Linderman notes that "in
both armies, eighteen-year-olds constituted the single largest

age group the first year of the war."[3] The men who served in the Union companies habitually referred to themselves as the boys, as did their officers and civilians, and nobody seems to have taken offense at the term. (For that matter, the term "infantry" itself comes from *fanti*—boys.) Laforest Dunham, having referred to a fellow soldier as a boy, admitted "but he is a married man." Then he explained, "We are all boys heare." What strikes us now is how elderly Civil War armies were compared to the ones produced by mass conscription in the twentieth century; more than three-fifths of the men enlisting were over twenty-one, and the median age of the northern soldier was the same as Cyrus Boyd's in 1860: twenty-four. But nonetheless, from 1861 to 1865, many American men spent the period of late adolescence and early adulthood usually associated with coming of age in the army.[4]

Cyrus F. Boyd felt the change begin in his initial weeks of service. The first sign that the young soldier was entering man's estate may have come from the flattering attention of the young women both back home and in other Iowa towns. In his diary Boyd began noting how well the girls treated him. The company was mustered in Keokuk, and there Boyd could scarcely make up his mind which young lady appealed to him most—"very shy" Lizzie Sullivan, whose eyes were "sparkling black," or the Johnston girls, who gave him and his friends gingersnaps when the regiment went down river. When attending church, he principally noticed the women; "The people are very sociable—especially the young ladies who seem to take a great interest in the soldiers." All of his stepping out with Maggie, Aggie, and Lizzie seems to have been given zest by the fact that he was a soldier soon to be off to the war. One night, "We had a good dinner and a pleasant time not unmarred however by the ever present thought this might be the *last* time we should meet these kind people." The romantic soldier paying court before the army moves on was a role that Boyd took to with no trouble. While it may have marred the

good times, it also added to their appeal. On the day the regiment boarded the boat that began the journey to the battle of
Shiloh, they marched down the Main Street of Keokuk under
the eyes of the women of the town. "1000 strong we marched
that afternoon in the pride and glory of youthful soldiers. The
sound of the music—the cheering shouts of the people robbed
[us] of all regrets and we marched proudly away. I saw some of
our good friends on the side walks—but it would not do to
look back."[5]

Another northern soldier, Thomas Evans, remembering
as a veteran less than a year later, also recognized a strong
element of the poseur in his departure for the front: "We
jogged along very merrily casting an occasional solemn look
back on the smoky hills among which was our recent home."
Their solemnity was mitigated by their new status: "it would
not do to be sad for we were soldiers and then to be a soldier
was to be something more than common people could boast
of. . . . Consequently our grief at parting was soon lost in the
contemplation of Future Glory that must await us. We supposed the war would only be of short duration and in our view
we were soon to return and then bearing the name of a soldier
would lift us above all common people."[6]

While Cyrus Boyd and other decent young men were
sparking the local girls, other Iowa soldiers enjoyed the sa-
loons and brothels of Keokuk. Boyd complained of their fas-
cination with the pleasures of the river town. But these unre-
pentant soldiers were claiming man's estate just as Boyd was,
although in less respectable ways. These young men asserted
their freedom from home and their new sense of masculinity
directly with whiskey and prostitutes. Soon Boyd recognized
that this type of coming of age would be typical of his fellow
soldiers, although he never learned to approve. "Whiskey and
sexual vices," he claimed, "carry more soldiers off than the
bullet."[7]

This escape from small town morality seemed to be an

inescapable part of soldiering. Old soldiers told a young recruit in another part of the Union army that "unless a man can drink, lie, steal, and swear he is not fit for a soldier." The men who pursued these vices and others—gambling and swearing were even more commonplace than drinking and fornication—disturbed Cyrus Boyd most by their enthusiasm: "How eager they seem to abandon all their early teachings and to catch up with everything which seeks to debase." Entering into the heavily masculine world of the army, they prided themselves on these thoroughly masculine vices. Gambling, drinking, and whoring were the traditional military vices as well. But to Boyd, who believed that true manhood required not release but restraint, the speed of his fellow soldiers degradation was appalling.[8]

Part of masculinity was achieving a self-discipline within the institutional discipline of the army. Cyrus F. Boyd and other northerners were as proud of their ability to withstand the temptations to which other soldiers gave in as they were of their service to the Union. Indeed, virtuous self-discipline was in itself a kind of service. When secession and rebellion became seen as hot-headed and impulsive—the result of unrestrained passion—self-discipline had political implications. During the war with the emotional, treacherous—feminine, childlike—South, the son of the rational, loyal—masculine, adult—North should be manly and upright.[9]

Yet part of the transformation necessary to become a soldier was hardening. While Boyd worried about men whose morals coarsened, he himself became less sensitive than he had been, more inured to suffering—both his own and others. Hardening was a process that ranged over all aspects of Boyd's life, from the commonplace to the most serious. It included getting used to a variety of discomforts and privations. His diet became coarser and simpler: "We have bid farewell to Bakers bread, cow's milk and such soft things. Had a piece of meat and a hard tack for breakfast—we are gradually breaking in." He learned to live outdoors; on the company's first night camping, "some of the boys began to think of their *mothers* and to talk of returning to their comfortable homes in the western counties."[10]

Hardening also included becoming accustomed to death and violence. The Fifteenth Iowa Infantry's introduction to bloodshed was perhaps more sudden than most. They were aboard a steamer at Pittsburgh Landing, having breakfast, when the order came to go ashore. Once there, they ran into the battle of Shiloh. They hurried for three miles, "meeting hundreds—yes thousands of men on the retreat who had thrown away their arms and were rushing toward the Landing—most of these were *hatless* and had nothing on them except their clothes." Some of those who fled had been shot; some ran and others were being carried off on stretchers. As they passed, the Iowans could not help noticing that some of the men were "covered with blood from head to foot."

"Here we were a new Regt which had never until this morning heard an enemies gun fire thrown into this *hell* of a battle—without warning." This was what the Civil War generation and others before and since called "the baptism of blood"—a phrase that connoted not only sudden and complete maturation but a radical transformation in character and experience. In telling his story, Boyd deliberately contrasted the innocence of the recruits to the horror of the baptism.

The general horror of battle quickly became more specific. The Fifteenth Iowa came to the edge of a large field with a ravine at one end. They crossed the ravine and deployed into line of battle, all in clear view of the Confederates. The rebels fired on them. "Here I noticed the first man shot. . . . He was close to us and sprang high in the air and gave one groan and fell *dead*." Then the hardening began. Boyd and his fellow soldiers each had to step over the newly dead man: "Each man as he came up seemed to hesitate and some made a motion to pick him up." But they could not stop to tend to the man.

Instead, the officers "sternly" ordered a charge, the men responded with a cheer, and they moved forward—only to be pushed back and to retreat over that same open ground. Masculinity meant restraining both their instincts to flee—to be a coward was to be no man—and their instincts to minister to the corpse.

As they were recrossing the field, a soldier came to Boyd and told him that they were leaving his brother Scott behind. Exhausted, Scott had collapsed on the ground. Boyd ran back to rescue his brother, only to be told "he never could go any farther and that I had better save myself and let him go." Pleading with his brother had no effect, so Cyrus Boyd grabbed Scott Boyd "by the *nap of the neck* and jerked him upon his feet and told him to *come* or I should help him with my *boot*." Scott stood up and, Cyrus helped him seek cover in the ravine. There he left his brother, confident he could work his way to safety, and returned to his company.

They continued to fight and fall back, ending up on the bluffs back at the landing where they had disembarked that morning. From the bluffs, they witnessed the arrival of Buell's army—all, in Boyd's opinion, that saved Grant, his army, and themselves. There was a final rebel charge but the Union forces held. Then came night, in many ways more horrible than the day had been. As the rain came down, Boyd and his company tried to sleep, listening to the groans of the other men, wounded and dying, who surrounded them, and to the sounds of wounded horses "running through the darkness." Morning came, and they were thankful to be held in reserve through the second day's fighting.

After the battle was finally over, Boyd and his friends went out and examined the field where they had fought. In just a few days war had changed them forever: "By this time we had become accustomed to seeing *dead* men and the *shock* had passed." They walked unmoved through the camp of the 52nd Illinois, looking at the bodies of dead and wounded soldiers,

Union and Confederate, "alternately scattered over the ground." Some of the wounded were "so near dead from exposure they were mostly insane." Elsewhere on the field, Boyd came across a dead rebel lying "on his back with his hands raised above his head"; the man "had died in great agony." Boyd reached down and, for a memento, took a button off his coat.

"War is *hell* broke loose and benumbs all the tender feelings of men and makes of them *brutes*." This was one conclusion Boyd drew after experiencing battle—presumably he included himself in his observations. He also concluded, "I do not want to see any more such scenes and yet I would not have missed this for any consideration." Being a man meant risking horrors that might unman a man—not by feminizing him but by making him inhuman. The hardening process was painful but it was well begun.[11]

Boyd noticed his own hardening most when it centered on his reaction—or growing lack of reaction—to suffering and death. He also found himself, despite his fears of moral degradation, taking food—chickens, pigs, roasting ears—from southern civilians. This was a more assertive form of masculine behavior than that which usually characterized the modest Boyd: being one of a group of armed men invading a homestead and taking what they wanted because nobody there could stop them. For Boyd, this food was due to the soldiers because they were loyal and self-sacrificing, while southerners were neither, and because, well, because they were soldiers. But he still responded to peacetime values that held foraging was theft. When Company E slaughtered a rebel sheep, Boyd noted approvingly that, "Major Purcell gave them a healthy old lecture and told the men they would not be allowed to *kill sheep* even if they were away from *home* and that hereafter such men would be severely *punished*."[12]

Finally, the hardening required a kind of mental vigor. Even as he inveighed against whisky and fornication, Boyd believed the real enemy to the soldier was internal: "More men *die* of homesickness than all other diseases—and when a man gives up and lies down he is a *goner*." His strategy for surviving the war was not simply military discipline—the ability to march, fight, obey orders, and keep oneself clean—not just moral discipline—the avoidance of temptation and degradation—but mental discipline as well. "Keep the mind occupied with something new and keep *going all the time* except when asleep." This pursuit of action and another duty that sounds a lot like positive thinking were required by manliness.[13]

That Cyrus F. Boyd should look back and choose to shape his life in the Union army into a tale of his coming of age is hardly surprising. His understanding of manhood, with its complex layers of definition, was commonplace among northerners of the Civil War era. Another veteran, Rice C. Bull, later said of his first battle—which was followed by several days spent wounded and a prisoner—"We had started out as boys with all the enthusiasm and ardor of youth; we had returned feeling that we were men, that the dividing line between boyhood and manhood had been passed by us on the field of Chancellorsville." Ideas about true manliness were central to the experience of northern men enlisting in the army, serving through the war, and remembering their service. In fact, the image of the young soldier coming of age was so central to later understanding of the war that it became, through a kind of cultural metonymy, a figure for both true manhood and for the nation itself.[14]

Becoming a man was no simple step for a middle class northerner like Cyrus F. Boyd. Sexual assertion by itself was insufficient; indeed, the young man might regard it as a sign that he was unmanly because he failed to exercise manly restraint. Physical violence—hunting and killing his fellow man in what seemed to be an extension of a primitive, perhaps savage, role—might be masculine, but true manhood required self-discipline and civilized morality. Both sexuality and violence had to be domesticated before a male became a true man—the one could be fulfilled only within the family, the other had to be directed purposefully toward a licensed enemy. Yet the demands of familial duty—defending family, home, and country—threatened to undercut the emotive ties that should bind a man to wife, parents, children, and friends: could a man harden himself enough to survive the war yet remain a son and a husband? True men recognized the role of emotions. An Illinois soldier confessed to his wife, "I cannot sing yet those songs such as, the vacant chair, the tears come." He went on, however, to invoke the ideal of manliness to justify his tears. "A man that cannot shed a tear when he thinks of those he left at home, is no man." Shedding a tear might be easy or painful or meaningless; what should a man do when his brother is lying exhausted on the battlefield of Shiloh while his company is rushing on? Is he first a sergeant or a sibling?[15]

Volunteering in itself was a sign of coming into manhood—it meant accepting a man's duties to defend his home and country. It was also, for many soldiers, the first time they had been away from parental supervision. Besides, military service had long been regarded as a metamorphosis. Sidney O. Little, an Illinois soldier, sounded as if he doubted his mother could believe in his transformation—he told her, "you may think me jesting"—but he assured her that "my coming into this war has made a man of your son." As Benjamen F. Ashenfelter put it, as he decided not to simply enlist but reenlist in August 1863, "A man that is afraid to face his Countries foe on an open field would not Defend A wife & children from the Midnight Assassin." Predictably, another attitude toward the relationship of soldiering and manliness was the claim that those who refused to fight were not men at all—they might as well be women. As one soldier said, "Any young man who is drafted now and forgets his manhood so far as to hire a substitute is'nt worthy the name of man and ought to be put in petticoats immediately." When the soldier Wilbur Fisk, an

unofficial correspondent of his newspaper back home, explained why he sometimes wrote at length on the minutiae of
soldier life, he spoke to the children of the community: "I
thought perhaps some of the boys who read the *Freeman,* but
are not old enough yet themselves to be soldiers, and some of
the little girls too, perhaps, who never can be soldiers, but who
almost wish sometimes they had been born boys so that they
could, would be interested to read all about the little affairs in a
soldier's common everyday life."[16]

Dye Davis, a soldier in the 48th Pennsylvania Volunteers,
liked to drink and brawl. James Wren, his captain, appealed to
notions of manhood to domesticate Davis. After one drunk,
Davis sobered up to find himself tied to a board. He requested
that the captain come to him, but Wren put the soldier off.
When Wren finally did visit Davis, he told him he would not
release him from his humiliation: "You told me before that you
would keep sober and be a man. There's no man in you."
Davis's reply was not a denial of the charge or a promise to
reform. Instead, he cried out, "O what would my Mary say if
she saw me here?" That, Wren approvingly noted, was when
Davis "commenced to be a [man]." The captain seized the
moment and used Davis's insecurity about his manhood. Wren
told Davis, "What would your Mary—your Mary would be
just like me. When she married you, she thought she had a
man and when I enlisted [you] I thought I had a man, but we
ware both mistaken." Weeping, Davis now told the captain,
"[I] will show you I will be a man." The captain judged Davis
to have kept his promise—he was wounded three times and
killed at the Wilderness. "A braver and better soldier than
Davis was not to be found in the service . . . but his Mary
was the great coard to be touched." What Mary Davis thought
of exploiting her husband's love for her to make him a better
soldier can only be conjectured, but Wren was hardly being
cynical—his definition of manhood encompassed loving husband and devoted soldier.[17]

Soldiers and other northerners frequently talked about fighting for the Union in specifically familial terms. Burage Rice, a New York captain, predicted the sure defeat of rebellion: "By the sacrifice and blood of our fathers was the Republic founded and by the treasure, faith, honor, and blood of their sons shall the same glorious flag forever wave over us." After the war, another New Yorker, Rice C. Bull, explained the volunteering by his generations by saying "that we felt that if our country was to endure as a way of life planned by our fathers, it rested with us children to finish the work they had begun." The Union was a fragile legacy handed down by the fathers of the revolutionary generation; their sons owed it protection.[18]

But the long chain of familial responsibility did not end with the current generation. The soldier's manhood required him to be a dutiful father as well as an obedient son. Henry H. Seys attributed his patriotism to "all the teachings of my boyhood—the very milk that nourished me in my infancy." This childhood education forced him to serve; otherwise "I should despise myself and be *ashamed to answer the questions of my children.*" Preserving the Union was the duty he owed both the generation behind him—particularly, it would seem, his mother—and the generation to come. He further told his wife, "teach our children that their duty to the land of their birth is next to their duty to their God. And that those who would desert *her* in the hour of danger, should be deserted by Him when *their* final calamity comes." Fathers expected mothers to inculcate their children with patriotic values; the feminine, domestic sphere was the ground for the masculine, public world.[19]

Henry H. Seys—and many others like him—saw himself as part of an extensive family, one that included generations of Americans, not just his own parents and children. To put it simply, many northerners considered the Union itself a family.

Fighting for the Union was, in that sense, much like fighting for one's family.

The familial metaphor influenced more than just the experience of the young men of the North who joined the Union army. It underlay a lot of thinking about the Union's war goals. One way to sum up Union war motivations succinctly was to say, the South needed to be taught a lesson. The North was the schoolmaster, the army the rod, and the South the disobedient child. The Vermont Yankee Wilbur Fisk, looking back in 1894, remembered the enthusiasm with which "we boys" had greeted the war: "We were ready to shout hurrah because now there would be a chance to teach the South a lesson, but we didn't realize how much it would cost us to teach it."[20]

Americans had a habit of talking about the body politic in terms of family relationships. Even anti-war northerners used familial imagery—"let the erring sisters depart in peace." Sisterhood, in this case, wasn't powerful—the image provoked a sad aura of weakness. Northerners who were pro-war used the image of unruly children who had to be made to obey. Sometimes this way of thinking about the South even reached the battlefield. Usually the specific familial imagery was hidden—northerners discussed southerners in terms of irrationality, emotion, savagery. One soldier wrote after the battle of Shiloh, "We showed them on the 2d day that northern obstinacy and coolness was more than a match for southern impetuosity"—obstinacy and coolness making up a critical part of manliness. Occasionally, northern imputations of southern childishness could be heard clearly. Henry C. Metzger wrote his sister, "I hate to hear the Rebles cheerre when they make a charge, they put me in mind of small schoolchildren about the time school is out." And indeed, sometimes men at war sounded as if they had schoolboy notions of honor behind all the bloodshed and policy. A perfectly sensible Wisconsin soldier wrote his wife this, as he visited with defeated Confederate soldiers in John-ston's army in 1865. "They are willing to admit that we have whipped them, and that is all that we want of them, is to acknowledge that we are too much for them, and we will also get along very finely." The soldier knew that behind the war had been issues of the nature of the American republic, the fate of democratic institutions, the place of slavery in a free society—yet he was able to write as if getting the Confederates to cry uncle had been the whole point of the war.[21]

The family analogy for understanding southern rebellion and northern response—the notion that the southern states might best be understood as disobedient children, the north-ern ones as filial—was woefully inadequate, indeed nonsensi-cal. I am not suggesting that anyone who seriously thought about politics entertained it for a minute or ever pushed the analogy into an identification. But in a period when political duties were so often expressed in familial imagery, it is striking that an armed rebellion of grown men was sometimes made to sound like a squabble in a kindergarten. The family provided the basis by which people thought about the political world.

Volunteer soldiers were both dutiful sons of their parents and of their revolutionary forefathers. Rebels challenged the mild parental authority of the national government—and thus defied the revolutionary generation as well. In that sense, the good sons of 1861 went to war against the bad sons. Perhaps there is a hint of this, however attenuated, in the way we continued to call the Civil War "the Brothers' War." And if there is not, at least there is little doubt we still think of the war as a family tragedy.

Thinking about the Civil War experience as a rite of pas-sage also continued into the next generation, as the sons of 1861 became the fathers of the Gilded Age. Once war becomes the defining experience for manhood, how can sons grow up in its absence? Just as the sons and grandsons down the line of the Revolutionary generation knew that they might never measure up to the heroes of 1776, the children of the postwar era faced the knowledge that the ultimate courage was shown not by them but by their fathers. (Or perhaps worse—as in the lifelong case of Theodore Roosevelt—had not been shown by their fathers.) Mrs. C. E. McKay, a Civil War nurse, said in 1876, "And ought we not carefully to teach the children of the present generation,—charging them not to let their children or their children's children forget what it cost their fathers to leave to them a united country."[22]

Men who had suffered through and survived the war told their children that military experience was crucial to manhood—in fact, spoke of war not only as a burden to be borne manfully but as a piece of luck. "Through our great good fortune," Oliver Wendell Holmes, Jr., said, "in our youth our hearts were touched with fire." An old man looking back, Leander Stillwell, remembered that after a year of war, "Our faces had insensibly taken on a stern and determined look, and soldiers who a little over a year ago were mere laughing, foolish boys, were now sober, steady, self-relying men." Stillwell's conclusion: "We had been taking lessons in what was, in many important respects, the best school in the world." Both the veterans and the younger men coming after them worried that with no equivalent experience, the youth of America would never grow into men. College athletics—played, at Harvard, on Soldier's Field—were just one way that postwar society tried to reproduce the manly experience of war for their children. Stephen Crane, in his great novel *The Red Badge of Courage* imaginatively seized the Civil War—and can we not hear, in its subtle ironies, a rebellious protest against turning frightened young men into heroes? Theodore Roosevelt literally seized upon war, pursuing the strenuous life up the slope of Kettle Hill. It took a generation of men uncertain of their manhood to find in the quick and nasty war with Spain in 1898 "a splendid little war."[23]

Talking about and presumably thinking about Civil War

soldiers coming of age eventually influenced thinking about the war itself. Some have seen—and do see—the Civil War as a coming-of-age experience for the nation entire. The war unified the country; it created strong institutions, including a powerful if short-lived army, and a long-lived sense of American power; it made Ohioans and New Yorkers as well as South Carolinians and Alabamians realize that they were Americans. It is as if the nation could not really mature without a massive bloodletting inflicted on itself, as if six hundred thousand deaths were some kind of adolescent rite of passage.

And Cyrus F. Boyd? He completed the romance of war by returning to Keokuk after Appomattox and marrying Maggie Johnston, one of the young ladies who had presented him gingersnaps. He had already become a soldier and an officer. Becoming a husband and a father—becoming in that sense as well, a man—was for him part of his Civil War experience. Nothing in the diary he left us suggests that he would have been surprised that his years spent fighting for the Union could be interpreted as years he spent growing up. That amalgam he and the culture that shaped him had already endorsed. He wrote as if the war that swept down on him and his companions was as natural and expected and necessary as childbirth, love, and death. This synchrony of public and private lives was how a generation of soldiers—and their children who followed—made sense of the painful, fumbling, demotic heroism and the remarkable unremarkableness of the men who fought for the Union.

2

The Northern Soldier
and His Community

IN sorrow and in anger, Lt. George Kies wrote his wife in
Connecticut from Baltimore, where his company was stationed. "I received a letter from som one yesterday purporting
to be from you but i cannot think that you would write me
such a letter." His wife scolded him for not writing to her, but
he had sent her letters. His wife accused him of involvement
with another woman with whom he had clandestine ren-
dezvous in Philadelphia. She thought he had spent the money
they needed to buy their children's gravestones on furs for the
other woman. These accusations were so detailed that Kies
could only conclude somebody was deliberately telling lies to
create trouble for him with his wife. "The one who says I hav is
a liar and i would tell them so though [they] are as big as
Christ himself." Whoever it was, it upset Kies that his wife
believed others instead of him. They had told her that he was
telling women that his wife was dead and that he was not a
married man. "you say that the soldiers say that i did not take
your Death very hard. If you will tell me what soldiers told that
i will let you know how hard they will take there [own]

19

Death." His wife's economic well-being worried him; he offered to send her all his pay and to steal his living. The lieutenant also sent his wife gifts.

But Kies's letters home indicate that derogatory reports from the front and his wife's accusations continued after she received his explanations and presents. He protested, "i hav not touched a woman since i was with you not so much as to feel of her Leg." His wife's charges of infidelity particularly bothered him because he currently suffered from sexual desire: "i do awfully want to som times and think that i should not care what become of me in the morning if i could sleep with you one night and have as good times as we used to in each others armes. I suppose you want it somtimes. i do when I think of you and that Pretty Leg of yours. . . ." Mrs. Kies had relented enough to send him her picture; it brought to his mind "so many pleasant recollection[s]."[1]

George Kies's troubled correspondence with his wife should serve us as more than an interesting, even juicy tidbit of the Civil War era or even than a reminder that Victorians had sex lives. Lt. Kies's preoccupation with his domestic life in the midst of war warns us of the danger of neglecting the personal when seeking the meaning of the Civil War experience. Specifically, this exchange of letters demonstrates the way in which information, gossip, sentiment, and acrimony passed back and forth between the men in the army and the people at home. This nexus of personal communication was a context in which men experienced the more purely military aspects of the war. Furthermore, it provided much of the motivation that kept men in the service of their country and their homes.

Recently a number of historians have turned their attention to the question of the motivations and experiences of the soldiers and citizens of the Civil War era. People who typically keep few written records left behind a profusion of letters, diaries, and memoirs for the years 1861 to 1865; the so-called inarticulate became voluble. These materials permit students of the war years to examine the attitudes of mid-nineteenth-century Americans, looking for new keys to the bloodiest puzzle in our history. Military historians, particularly those influenced by John Keegan's *Face of Battle,* have also developed a fresh concern with what makes soldiers fight; they too have started to turn to the lavish records of the war years to understand the American soldier.[2]

In this chapter, I will consider the ways that his ties with his home influenced the experience of the northern soldier during the war. While combat, military discipline, ideology, and leadership have all been evaluated as determinants of soldier conduct during the war, community values were equally important. In fact, they were crucial to the way in which Americans made war from 1861 to 1865. Since the war itself can be viewed as a conflict over the meaning of community, this should not be surprising. The closeness of the soldier to his community both undercut the traditional arrangements that armies make for discipline and provided a powerful impetus for military service and patriotic tenacity.

In many ways American armies during the Civil War contravened normal military practice. The process by which men are turned into soldiers—one is tempted to say "reduced to soldiers"—involves removing them from the larger society. They wear distinctive dress, distinctive haircuts, submit to unusual drill, discipline, and ritual, are commanded by officers. They are literally regimented. Armies master people by subjecting them to unfamiliar environments; people adapt to their new environments and thus become soldiers. Armies work by setting men apart.[3]

To a large extent, Civil War armies succeeded in doing these things. The volunteers did become soldiers. But the transformation from civilian to soldier was rarely completed. One reason for this is that in some ways the company—the basic military unit—functioned as an extension of the soldier's home community. In most ways, a soldier's company was the army for that soldier. Within his company he received his orders, his supplies, his companionship. Companies and regiments were raised by local leaders in specific towns and counties; the soldier's officers and fellow soldiers were most often men he had known all his life. In the midst of military life, the soldier was constantly reminded of his civilian life. Unlike the French Foreign Legion, the Union Army would have been a wretched institution for any man trying "to forget" to join—unless he joined up away from his home.[4]

It is important to realize that this way of recruiting and organizing soldiers was not simply accidental. Instead, this voluntary organization of small communities into a national army, the amalgamation of civic pride and national patriotism, serves as an example of how the volunteers imagined the Union should function. In 1861, a Union which went to war by creating a centralized army would have been unrecognizable to them. The local nature of the companies and regiments faithfully mirrored the body politic at large.

For new recruits, the army should be a terrifying institution; soldiering should be different from anything they have known before. Like all institutions, established armies have traditions of their own. A Scottish recruit coming to a British regiment or even an American teenager entering the cadet corp at West Point would find himself bound—and inspired—not only by formal discipline but by the powerful traditions, history, and myths of his new home. These traditions too play their role in transforming civilians into soldiers. But in most cases Civil War regiments had no such traditions. These were new regiments, making up their regimental traditions. The new soldiers themselves were far more intimately involved in the creation of these traditions, in the interpretation of company history than is ordinarily the case—indeed, than would be the case for conscripts coming to the armies after 1863.

Civil War companies were first and foremost military institutions, but they were not exempt from the culture of the nineteenth-century American volunteerism that produced them. Sometimes soldiers insisted that their company—their new home—serve other functions. They might form societies "for mutual improvement in cultivating the mind" or for debating important questions of the day, such as whether or not "education has more influence over the mind of man than money." Bible classes held in an Indiana regiment paid special attention to the conflicting claims of Calvinism and Arminianism. Soldiers would donate money to buy their regiments libraries, organize Christian associations, or hold Sunday prayer meetings—all as if they had read Tocqueville. Companies of Union volunteers, then, behaved much as other American fraternal organizations. The average Civil War company began with all the discipline of a lodge of Elks.[5]

Armies deliberately create distance between a soldier and his officers. Generally, officers come from a different class from the soldiers'—historically, from an aristocratic class. The army feeds, clothes, and arms officers differently, pays them more, educates them to a higher level. Officers are given legal sanctions for their authority, authority they can ultimately back up with the death penalty. In theory, all of these factors combine to legitimate the authority of the officer corps over the rank and file.[6]

During the Civil War, a soldier's immediate officers hardly came from a hereditary caste. They were generally his fellow townspeople or local men prominent in his county. They might have the prestige of organizing the company and back home they may have been men of reputation and power. They were also men that the soldier had probably known all his life and men he had trouble thinking of as his superiors in anything but the incidentals of rank.

Officers rapidly became aware of the problem that the local nature of military units posed for discipline. In 1861 Major Charles S. Wainwright noted "how little snap men have generally." His regiment's officers, even though they were well thought of, could not "get fairly wakened up." "Their orders come out slow and drawling, then they wait patiently to see them half-obeyed in a laggard manner, instead of making the men jump to it sharp, as if each word of the order was a prod in their buttocks." He blamed this state of affairs in part on customary small-town indolence; he also blamed the process by which companies were organized—"the officers having raised their own men and known most of them in civil life." "I am every day more and more thankful that I never laid eyes on a soul in the regiment until I joined it." As late as 1864, another New York officer, George Anthony, greeted new recruits for his battery with mixed feelings when they turned out to be men from his county: "I would never take command of neighbors as soldiers again. And the higher the quality of the men the more such a command is to be dreaded." Even soldiers themselves might identify this as a problem. When mismanagement by the quartermaster led to a shortage of rations in one regiment, one soldier, who a few weeks earlier had complained of strict discipline, attributed the inefficiency to the fact that affairs were run on a volunteer basis: "The officers have no dignity & the men no subordination."[7]

The threat to discipline posed by the community came from others than just the soldiers themselves. The community kept in close touch with the companies it sent to war. Newspaper articles reported their exploits, homefolk sent and received letters, soldiers returned home on furloughs, and civilians even visited their friends and family in the army. The reenforcement of local values that this constant communication permitted could run counter to military values. When Captain John Pierson told his wife that his soldiers were probably writing home he was a tyrant, he was not alone. Officers usually planned to return to their communities when the war was over; the way they treated their neighbors and their neighbors' sons would be remembered. Letters home were not all the problem either. Because citizens visited their friends in camp, they could interfere with military values right on the spot. In one Massachusetts regiment the soldiers welcomed their colonel's decision to limit drill: his wife on a visit had told him that he drilled the men too hard. The community never entirely relinquished its power to oversee its men at war.[8]

As unfamiliar as the military experience was to most northern soldiers, the presence of friends and even brothers, uncles, or cousins, the frequent communication with those at home, and the ad hoc nature of the volunteer army served to make it more familiar than is typical of armies. Small-town mores were an impediment to military discipline as classically understood. The constant reminders of home provided men with an alternate set of values and diminished the authority of their officers—men who were equally imbued with civilian values in any case. Yet at the same time small-town mores reduced soldiers' military efficiency, they also worked as the glue of this citizen army. If community values helped make the Union soldier a difficult one to command, they also helped make him as good a soldier as he turned out to be.

First, soldiers believed that they were fighting for their families and communities. The homefolk had sent them to war. Rallies, public meetings, exhortations from the press and pulpit had encouraged the teenagers and men of the North to enlist; their communities presented them with homemade American flags, promised always to remember their bravery, and marched them out of town to the accompaniment of brass bands. The question why parents and wives seemed so eager to sacrifice their menfolk is a troubling one, but it is clear that their influence helped persuade many men to volunteer. To be a good son, a good brother, a good husband and father, and to be a good citizen meant trying to be a good soldier.[9]

The call of home could, of course, unravel a soldier's morale. Silas W. Browning confessed to his wife, "I have not shad tears but twice since I left Home & that was when I received your letters." One Philadelphia soldier lamented, "I supoze I wont hardly know Phila when I get to see it." He was moody when he wrote because the new homesick recruits were playing "Home Sweet Home." "They get in their tents and practice it all day. . . . I dont like to hear it for it makes me feel queer." A preacher's sermon on "the dear ones at home" could start veterans crying. A New Jersey soldier claimed that in the trenches around Petersburg soldiers literally died from homesickness. But as long as soldiers were sure that those they most missed believed in them and the cause for which they fought, their love for home stimulated their support for the Union.[10]

Second, soldiers knew that their behavior while in service was monitored by the folks back home. The army provided little escape from the prying eyes of small-town America. News of a man's conduct, moral and military, was too easily sent home. And home is where the volunteer expected to return when the war was done. As mentioned earlier, there was a surprising amount of communication between the soldiers and their homes—both through letters and furloughs—and this kept soldiers informed of the expectations of the loved ones left behind. Soldiers wanted to meet these expectations; they wanted to be able truthfully to write home that they had done their duty.

Furthermore, the soldier himself was not the only one in close communication with his townspeople. His officers and fellow soldiers also wrote their loved ones and went home on furlough. They could report his behavior—or misbehavior—to the folks at home. This communication created powerful constraints on soldiers' conduct. Discipline, bravery, perseverance, and good morals all could represent an attempt to maintain the respect of civilian society as well as adaptation to front-line conditions.

"Write often and all the news and how everything is getting along even to the cats & dog, hogs and everything else you can think off." So requested Albertus Dunham in the fall of 1862. Another soldier filled his letters home with questions such as, "How many bushalls of onions did that pach yield?" Information and opinions circulated easily among soldiers in camp and people back at home. For example, soldiers read each other's mail. If a soldier's family sent him news from home—or better still, a newspaper from home—it might circulate throughout his company until the letter or newspaper was all worn out. And men took rumors and hometown opinion seriously. One soldier wrote his parents that he and "the other boys were amazed that you heard that we were guilty of unworthy conduct." Denying the story, he asked who was spreading it. On the other hand, soldiers were not particularly reluctant to spread rumors themselves. One mother who warned her son always to speak respectfully of his officers received a defiant answer: "I intend to write just as I think they deserve and tell the truth and nothing but the truth." The son proceeded to do so. "Our captain is just as good as so much trash." He was far from being the only Union soldier who told tales on his officers and fellow soldiers.[11]

This reportage influenced soldiers' conduct in all aspects of their lives. For one thing, a man knew that his behavior on the battlefield would be reported to his community. Men oversaw each other's behavior in battle, and they sent home accounts of bravery and cowardice. Bravery was a virtue that would earn a soldier the respect of his community back home, not just his company, and cowardice its contempt. A man who skulked or ran faced not just ridicule from his comrades but a soiled reputation when he returned to civilian life. George Waterbury first tried to get put on the sick list and then deserted to avoid fighting in the Chancellorsville campaign; a fellow soldier sent the news back to Connecticut. When one captain dodged battle in 1862, a soldier under him broadcast his conduct: "He contrived to stumble, then gave out he was wounded in the knee, and called for a stretcher, was put on it, and carried a little ways when the carriers rested and the shells falling a little to thick for the Captain, he told them men to hurry up which they did not do, when up he jumped and beat the whole to the Hospital, after which we never saw him until we got upon this side of the Rappahannock."[12]

Soldiers demanded courage of their officers in a way they rarely did of their fellow soldiers. Soldiers who had enlisted under their company commanders had a right to feel particularly betrayed if their captains proved cowardly. After all, the officer who formed a company among his friends and neighbors promised them either implicitly or explicitly—usually the latter, and in most grandiloquent fashion—to lead them into battle. James K. Newton wrote home that the reputation of his captain's bravery at Shiloh "was all a hoax." On the contrary, the captain had disappeared when the battle began. "When asked where he was going he replied 'that he was going down to the river to *draw rations* so that the boys could have something to eat as soon as they were done fighting.'" Shortly after the battle, the captain resigned. Newton accused the captain of stealing the company funds as well as of cowardice. Perhaps Newton was wrong. But clearly an officer who resigned after his company had its first taste of combat laid himself open to the contempt of his men, contempt so great that Newton was ready to believe he was both a swindler and a shirker.[13]

During combat, could men think of their reputations? The answer is probably yes. Men wrote home how they thought of their loved ones even in the cannon's mouth; men did die with the names of their beloved on their lips. The desire to live up to the expectations of those at home reenforced natural bravery and military discipline in helping determine men's conduct on the battlefield. Leander Stillwell remembered that when his regiment turned and ran in his first battle, he kept thinking, "What will they say about this at home?" Nonetheless, combat has its own compulsions. The good opinion of the folks back home was probably more important in men's decision to continue their service.[14]

While courage in battle resulted from the moment's excitement, it took considerable more reassurance to stay in the army day after day, year after year. There were military compulsions; deserters could be shot. Many deserted successfully, however, and the so-called "bounty-jumpers" made a career of enlisting and deserting. The continual reassurance that those back home approved of one's service, a reassurance provided by letters—and painfully missed when letters did not come—was crucial to the soldiers. As long as the communities of the North supported the war effort, there would be northern soldiers in the ranks of the Union army.

Yet the hunger for a family's respect and admiration, the desire to satisfy those at home that one was a patriot and a hero, could be undercut by other duties that a man held. A man's patriotism had to compete with other equally important values; military service was possible when he believed that things were all right at home. Otherwise the claims of home threatened his devotion to the army.

Private William DeLong, considered one of the best soldiers in his regiment, could not helped being affected when a neighbor wrote him that his wife had been washing four to five days a week to earn money, became very sick, was "destitute of every Thing for her comfort and With out food or wood." Even though her neighbors had helped her with everything they could, she wanted him to get his pay and come home immediately. DeLong did not want to leave his company, but he did brood about his wife's sufferings. He brought the neighbor's letter to George Anthony, his commanding officer, who "assured him that this letter is unreliable," but who also immediately wrote to his brother back home, telling him to find out what Mrs. DeLong needed and buy it for her. The officer attested that DeLong felt "the sufferings of a true man" over the misery of his wife. Here lay the contradiction. A true man fought for the Union, which was indeed a way of fighting for his family. But a true man also sheltered his family. A man was expected to earn a living; a man was expected to protect and to support his family. Joining the army was an extension of the duty to protect one's family, but men anticipated that military service would support them as well. If it did not, their morale declined. New Yorker Hermon Clarke said, "I see men often after getting a letter from home go to the officers and enquire if there isn't some way to get pay. Their families write they are suffering for want of money; some are turned out of doors. All the officers can do is pity them, which only aggravates them."[15]

Sometimes the demoralization reached the point where soldiers would desert; they believed they had to go home and look after those whose claims were more immediate than those of the Union. For example, during the winter of 1863, infrequent paydays caused John E. Lowery to desert and do odd jobs—chopping wood and working at a lime kiln—to support his family until he was arrested and returned to his company. But when men felt certain that their families were looked after and that their desertion would shame both them and their families, the force of the community helped keep them in the army. By and large, this was the case for the northern soldier during the Civil War.[16]

Finally, gossip home included reports on men's moral behavior. David Seibert wrote his father indignantly that he had not been going with disreputable women, no matter what had been written about him. Laforest Dunham told his unmarried sister that a soldier who had visited his family, "a first trate fellow," was "one of these kind that is noted for these houses of ill fame and has a dissease that he never will get over by so doing." In varying measures of glee and shock, soldiers told of their officers having sex with prostitutes or other women; if these women were black or "yellow" it added additional cause for comment. "Good business for married men," one of them sardonically noted. Another told of his captain's desire to "stick close to a yalow girl after night"; surely the Captain "would improve the stock very much." This Presbyterian soldier informed on his captain because "i said when i left home that i would not write a lie home and i shall not do it."[17]

This is not to claim that northern soldiers always lived up to the dictates of Victorian morality. The army saw its share of gambling, drinking, smoking, and fornication. Even so, our more pungent discussions of these activities comes from the letters of moralistic soldiers. Men's behavior coarsened, but they did not lose the sense that there were moral standards by which they were expected to abide. Leander Stillwell, whose regiment ran at Shiloh, also got drunk early in his service. At first he enjoyed the sensation—"But it suddenly occurred to me that I was drunk, and liable to forever disgrace myself, and everybody at home, too." He hid in the woods until he sobered up. The pious Frederick Pettit praised "those home influences." "They will save many of our brave soldiers from a fate worse than death on the battlefield."[18]

Gerald Linderman calls courage, which is for him a cluster of values, many of them domestic, "the cement of armies." One could also say that the love of home was "the cement of armies." Small-town mores influenced the behavior of the men at war. Love of home helped keep men fighting for the long years of the war. Concern with reputation supplemented military discipline in camp, on the march, and in battle. The familiarity that so jeopardized discipline initially came from a set of shared values that helped mobilize the teenagers and men of the North, kept them in the army once they were there, and saw that they maintained a high standard of behavior. They were an individualistic society's substitute for militarism, a voluntary society's substitute for coercion.

> "I guess we all do things away from home we wouldn't do
> at home. And since most of us are never at home we're
> always doing things we would never do."
> *Fardiman, in Malcolm Bradbury's "Composition"*

While the constraints that community oversight placed on soldiers were powerful, they were not irresistible. As the war continued, soldiers necessarily became inured to discipline, hardship, and bloodshed. The ties that bound them to their homes rarely broke but often frayed. The distance between a soldier and his home helped encourage drastic changes in his behavior, even to the point of helping him create a new identity more appropriate to the conditions of war than of peace. There is no doubt that soldiers behaved in ways they never would have at home—otherwise they could not have been soldiers.[19]

Even though the tug toward home never lost its power over most soldiers, as the war continued veteran soldiers also felt a psychological distance grow that matched the physical distance between their camps and their homes. Part of the transformation from volunteer to soldier was a tendency to disassociate oneself from both one's former life and one's old community. But the distance also came from the soldier's growing fear that the community both no longer respected soldiers and no longer deserved a soldier's respect.

The soldiers had marched off hoping to become heroes; as the war went on they began to suspect they were the only set of heroes their hometowns were going to produce. Whatever the difficulties experienced by the civilians of the North, they looked insignificant to the men at the front. As towns scrambled to meet their quotas of soldiers or squabbled over wartime politics, soldiers wondered if most of their communities' patriotism had not left with them. Soldiers saw themselves as better embodying the values of the community than those who selfishly stayed behind; indeed, the center of moral authority shifted from the community at home to the community in arms, from the civilian fathers to the soldier sons.[20]

When soldiers cursed those who paid the commutation fee or fled the draft, they were not referring simply to some general set of cowards. They often had specific individuals in mind, former neighbors, fellow schoolboys, hometown rivals.

Henry Carroll asked his mother to tell "the Gentry" who planned to go to California to avoid the draft that "they had better make their calculation to stay when they go there." "The boys say when they get back they dont intend to let any such craven cowards and skulkers come back to enjoy the peace." The soldiers dismissed those who opposed the draft as cowards; those who opposed the war—the Peace Democrats or Copperheads—they called traitors. A Connecticut soldier, hearing that his hometown of New Milford supported the Democratic candidate for governor, said that he hoped he had no friends among the disloyal. Park H. Fryer, an Ohio soldier, supported the soldier-led mobs that sometimes destroyed the presses of newspapers of Peace Democrats: "I say go in Boys fight while you are at home as well as in the Field if you can find the enemy. . . . I could cock my Enfield at a Rebel at home just as cool as down here in dixy." Another Ohio soldier composed—or at least copied—a rhyming malediction directed at the Copperheads/—"Brazen faced Copperheads/ White livered Copperheads/ False-harted Copperheads"—of his township. Furthermore, in many cases the animosity directed at individuals broadened to include whole communities. Henry C. Bear lambasted Oakley, Illinois, where he imagined citizens advocated resisting conscription: "I suppose they would talk about resisting a Hurricane in their weakness and blindness, there in that God forsaken place." A soldier named Lyman Foster enunciated the ultimate and logical conclusion: "i say shoot the traiters at home & we will be all right[.]"[21]

Indeed, the constant intercourse with home played its role in creating distance. When away from home, soldiers felt neglected. When home on leave, some soldiers felt treated with disdain. The spectacle of life going on without them might be profoundly unsettling. The neglect or contempt, real or imagined, felt by soldiers angered and depressed them. Letters home kept the men in touch with those they left behind, but they also revealed the immense distance that grew up between the worlds of civilians and soldiers. When soldiers received letters complaining of the high price of black powder or how hard it was to buy silk dresses, they felt little sympathy. The seeming inability of the civilians to compare their lot with that of the soldiers infuriated men. One protested, "These persons do not consider us who are opposed to bullets and steal blades under dangerous hardships." Perhaps partially inspired by the magnificent irrelevance of the gripes from his hometown, this particular soldier deserted less than a year later. Desertion did not become the norm, but alienation did.[22]

Of course, some soldiers had never liked their hometowns to begin with. Leander Chapin expressed this sentiment when he advised his mother to leave their Connecticut home and move to Springfield, Massachusetts. *"I would not stay in aristocratic gossiping Enfield for an interest in Goshen."* He was glad when he left Enfield, and he "was glad that I do not as a soldier count on the quota of the town. . . ." Nor did all soldiers regret leaving their families behind. One soldier assured his father that he was sending him all the money he could spare, and told him not to share any of it with "that wife of mine if I must caule her wife."[23]

In general, however, a soldier's alienation reached its limits when it threatened his feelings toward his immediate family. The soldier exempted parents, children, wives, and sisters from his attacks on northern civilians, and even brothers, uncles, and male cousins usually got the benefit of the doubt when Copperheads and cowards were damned. The strongest claim that home had on a soldier was his family. It was a rare soldier who did not imagine peace as a return to his household.

Soldiers regularly claimed that it was only through leaving their homes and suffering through army life and the violence of war that they learned domesticity's true value. A soldier in Sherman's army, "heartily sick of this kind of life," longed for "a pleasant retreete from the repulsive scenes of this man slaughtering life"—"the society of my family in some secluded spot, shut out from the calamities of war." One officer contrasted the "bursting warm hearts love" of a boy who was willing to join the Regular army in order to get a furlough home with the "cold amphibious blood" of gentlemen who lounged in their clubs because they "vote home a bore." "This little boy was already a Veteran. . . . but in order once more to get home, to sit once more with his mother & sisters around the family hearth, this brave little boy was willing to bare his little Body to five years more of Battle and Hardship." The officer asked, "Is there anything that can more strongly than this, point out the great power and influence of Home?" "If I am spared to ever get home again I think I shale know how to appreciate [it]," one soldier wrote his wife and daughter. "I thought I had know it before but a man does not untill he gets in the army." Leaving home, then, was a precondition for knowing home.[24]

Home looked mighty good compared with the army. A song like "Just Before the Battle, Mother" served not only to express soldiers' deepest feelings—their longing for family and home—but also to instruct them as to what their feelings should be. Remembering home, dreaming of it, planning for an eventual return to it allowed men to focus on something other than the army and the war and thus to a certain extent retain their prewar identities. In most cases the lure of home was sufficient to prevent the civilian from being permanently submerged in the soldier.

Nonetheless, for the time being the soldier had to predominate. One soldier explained this by saying he belonged "to Uncle Sam, mentally, morally, and physically." His job, his duty, was to be a soldier. "My virtues and vice must correspond to that of my fellows; I must *lie* to rebels, *steal* from rebels and *kill* rebels." And if a man's duty called upon him to embrace deceit, theft, and murder, is it surprising that he also might fall prey to profanity, tobacco, women, and liquor? Particularly when he was away from home for the first and perhaps last time of his life? Community values reenforced the military regimen to discipline the Union soldier, but even in tandem they were not always successful. So the war to defend their communities led soldiers temporarily away from their community values.[25]

The logic of this war became such that in its last year some northern soldiers literally made war on the homes of their enemies. The intent of Sherman's march was to demoralize the southern people. Sherman said he proposed to make the southern people "feel that war and individual ruin are synonymous terms." The demoralization would spring from southern recognition that their government was helpless to protect them from Union soldiery and Union armies. Northern soldiers entered the homes of their southern counterparts, terrorized their wives, parents, and children, confiscated their food, and sometimes burned down their houses. Deserting Confederate soldiers, whose numbers swelled as their families' helplessness grew, affirmed the effectiveness of this policy. During the Atlanta campaign, one officer said of the southern people whom they impoverished, "it is but right that these people should feel some of the hardships of war, they will better appreciate peace when it does come. . . ." Much like home, the value of peace and the Union could best be learned—by southerners at least—in their absence.[26]

Sherman's men were a long way from home, in terms of time, distance, and often psychology. Emblematic of this is the perhaps trivial sounding fact that during the march and the campaign of the Carolinas, Sherman and his men could not receive any messages from home, any letters, any telegrams, any orders. Sherman himself testified to the freedom he felt when he cut the wire from Atlanta to Washington and knew the authorities could not stop him from undertaking the great march. Rarely had the northern soldier been so free from supervision as he was during the March to the Sea and through the Carolinas. He behaved with corresponding license and gusto. The fact that the countryside he traversed did not look, sound, or smell much like home also encouraged the soldier to treat its inhabitants and their property more harshly than he otherwise might have. The plantations he destroyed were built on slavery, an institution popularly portrayed as antithetical to family and home. The soldier also took revenge for his long absence from home by destroying the homes of Confederate soldiers.[27]

This assault, both symbolic and literal, on the southern home, provided an oddly fitting end to this war in defense of community values. For, finally, wasn't the Civil War a war over the meaning of home? It has often been called a fratricidal war, a war over who shall rule the home that was the American nation. Closer to the point, however, is the way the dispute between the North and the South was over the different concepts that people had of what this American home was. Lincoln had warned against "a house divided." When a northern recruit joined the army to protect American institutions, his idea of those institutions came from his own, usually limited experience. The institutions, the values for which he fought were those with which he had grown. Democracy meant the town hall, education meant the schoolhouse, Christianity meant the local church. As for broader concepts—freedom, Constitution, democratic rule—so frequently had they been mediated by local figures that even they might be thought of as community values. In the North, localism aided, not hindered, national patriotism. The northern soldier fought for home and for Union, for family and for nation. For him, the Civil War experience made sense only in relation to both the domestic and the civic components of his world.[28]

3

"The Boys":
The Problem of Authority

SERGEANT Cyrus F. Boyd hated Colonel Hugh T. Reid. When Boyd's company was formed of Indianola and Knoxville, Iowa, men, he lost the election for second lieutenant—the Knoxville men were in a majority, and Boyd was from Indianola—but he succeeded in obtaining the rank of orderly sergeant. Boyd not only was disappointed; he felt betrayed. His company was mustered in as part of the Fifteenth Iowa Volunteer Infantry; they first met Colonel Reid at dress parade. "After this Lieut Col Dewey introduced Hugh T Reid by saying, 'Boys, behold your Colonel,' and we *beheld* him."

Six months after Shiloh—a battle that led to the premature retirement of several officers—Boyd ran for lieutenant again and lost again, by three votes. Boyd's judgment of Hugh Reid's conduct at Shiloh was that the man was brave but incompetent. Boyd finally decided that Colonel Reid was generally incompetent. Then came the battle of Corinth, which affected Boyd's military career in contradictory ways.

Boyd's regiment was falling back. Boyd remembered that as the regiment "began to break," a soldier named Charley

Vinton "came staggering along by me." Vinton asked another soldier to help him but that soldier ignored him. So Boyd took Vinton's arm and brought him to a surgeon. "He was wounded not severely in the head but the blood covered him all over and he looked like one mortally wounded." Then Boyd joined the general retreat.

Besides wounding Charley Vinton, the battle of Corinth also killed the man who beat out Boyd in the last election. This time Boyd won the election for higher office—only to have Colonel Reid refuse to recommend him. Instead, Reid recommended that the governor of Iowa appoint a man whom Boyd dismissed as a "pie peddlar." When in camp, E. P. Bye baked pies and sold them to his fellow soldiers. Boyd confronted Reid, only to be told that he had disobeyed orders by helping Charley Vinton off the field at Corinth and so Reid had denied him his promotion. Two weeks after Bye received his commission, Boyd asked him into his tent and "told [him] *never* while he was in Co "G" to give me an order as I should never obey him and that I considered him a *sneaking puppy* and that [I] might consider his *hide* worth about *ten cents* in good currency." The new lieutenant assured Boyd he had not sought the office and intended to resign as soon as possible. Besides intimidating the new lieutenant, Boyd wrote to a friend raising a new Iowa regiment and asked for a transfer—but orders forbade enlisted men from transferring from one regiment to another. Other soldiers encouraged his discontent. They told him he was "the best Orderly in the Regt and the most abused man"—but they were most effusive when they were drunk and Boyd found the sympathy of drunks hard to take.

At least some of the other soldiers in the regiment shared Boyd's distaste for Reid. While in winter camp, they amused themselves by nocturnal assaults on his headquarters. All day long they would gather brickbats and once the night had come and the camp was sleeping, they snuck out "by platoons" and threw the missiles at the window of the room in which the colonel slept. When the outraged colonel emerged to order the guard to track them down, they were already back in their tents pretending to sleep. "Almost any man with two pennyweights of horse sense can in this state of affairs *trace* from *cause* to *effect*." About this time, Colonel Reid insisted that all the soldiers draw brand new uniforms—a serious drain on their monthly clothing allowance that meant some money would come out of most soldiers' pay. When supplies ran low and the men were reduced to bread and coffee, a soldier came out of the door of his tent and cried out, "More sowbelly and less style." The other soldiers joined him in his cry. And when the colonel tried to generate support of his officers' resolutions in favor of the Emancipation Proclamation, he found one quarter of the regiment voting against the resolutions and another quarter refusing to vote at all.

Boyd's difficulties with the colonel were finally resolved. His friend with the new regiment put Boyd in for not simply a transfer but a promotion. In the spring of 1863, Colonel Reid showed Sergeant Boyd a commission from the 34th Iowa Infantry which had come in for him. Reid told him that he had already sent in Boyd's name for a promotion within not only his own regiment but his own company. But Boyd replied that the colonel had had one chance to give him a promotion. "He smiled a kind of *Aligator smile* and I bid him an *Aligator adieu*." Nonetheless, as he prepared to go, he felt sad. He was leaving "those *faithful boys* with whom for 19 long months of suffering of trials and common misfortunes—amid hunger privations and scenes of peril and death we had stood together as one man." He realized that "I should rather be a non-commissioned officer with such *friends* than be at the head of any Regiment *without them*." He felt as if Colonel Reid had driven him from his home.[1]

Boyd's often-thwarted promotion had resonance beyond his individual case. One should remember, for example, that the Civil War occurred because the South refused to accept the democratic election of a President—thus, to most northerners at least, interfering with the democratic process itself. Reid was doing much the same thing. Worse, Reid was supporting the notion—fundamental to most militaries—that officers knew better than their men. He was attempting to act on this principle, however, in a culture where it was not a commonplace.

Officers were neither products of an aristocratic class with long traditions of military service nor, as a general rule, regular army men, trained to command professional soldiers. Those two models would not do to guide officers in the Civil War—although the second model was sometimes invoked and volunteer soldiers sometimes accused officers of trying on the first. Perhaps more important than the background of the officers was the background of northern soldiers. Almost none of these soldiers had regular army experience, and few of them came from any tradition of subservience. Furthermore, even though we often compare the industrial North with the agrarian South, few volunteers were products of "factory discipline."

Obviously there were exceptions. Most black regiments were recruited among southern freedmen—their soldiers had been schooled in slavery. Even so, in black regiments military hierarchy was reenforced both by racial hierarchy—officers were almost always white—and by more extreme military discipline—black soldiers suffered the full penalties of military discipline far more often than white soldiers did. Black soldiers had learned not just obedience in slavery but resistance as well—there were mutinies over the issue of pay. But they were so committed to the goal of emancipation that they possessed powerful ideological motivation for military duty. Immigrant soldiers, such as the Irish, might be said to have come from a tradition of subservience to aristocrats—yet Irish soldiers in particular were viewed as the worst discipline problems in the Union army: they came from a long tradition of resistance too. Furthermore, the immigrant soldier had all the resentments of culture and class. They were frequently looked down upon by their officers who were often Protestant while the soldiers were Catholic. Immigrant soldiers and black soldiers made up about one-third of the Union army. Relations between officers and men differed for these soldiers.[2]

What was the model of correct relations between officers and soldiers for the rest? One model was corporate and volunteeristic. Patriotic men had gathered together to save the Union. While they were so gathered, there would be necessarily officers and men among them. But this was a matter of expedience. The officer was no better than the soldier and the divisions between them, while useful, were artificial. That, of course, is the ideal model of how a democratic society makes war. Another model came from the domestic experience of mid-nineteenth-century Americans. This model was hierarchal. Officers were parents; soldiers were children. This model cut against the notion of an army of equals, but it radically differed from the notion that officers and men came from different castes. A father, after all, is not supposed to think of his children as scum. A father may command his children but he also keeps their best interests at heart. And while this model suited a democratic society less well than the first model, it also made intuitive sense. The institution in which men were most used to issuing orders and receiving them, the model for authority, was the family. When Lincoln relieved George McClellan, the commander of the Army of the Potomac, Paul Oliver, an officer, evoked familial imagery to convey the reaction of both officers and soldiers. He said, "We feel just like a huge family who has lost its father."[3]

The customary language of soldiers employed metaphors of youth and age. The soldiers in a company were sometimes "the men" but just as often "the boys." In many cases, naturally, the soldiers in a company were young men; many were under twenty. "The boys" also conveyed the flavor of camaraderie and informality—and something of the sense that in some ways this war was a great adventure. But it was also an oddly childish term for men engaged in grimly serious business. It did not seem to refer to adults who could make their own decision. This infantilizing term implied that soldiers needed adult guidance and governance.

But if the soldiers were "boys," they required affection as well. Besides the obvious fact that many officers grew genuinely fond of their men, Americans believed that a proper relationship between commanders and those commanded was one based on respect and concern. Captain Levi Kent acknowledged the affection that an officer could and he believed should develop toward the soldiers he commanded. He noted in his diary that, "I don't know how the other officers feel toward their companys, but my good Co F are head & ears above the others." This affection came purely from their joint work as soldiers. "Not a man among them that I ever knew before meeting them at Camp Green and I know there is not a man among them that would like to be transferred to any other company in the Regt." Kent understood his affection to be reciprocated. The mutual affection was both a product of the kindly treatment to which he insisted the soldiers were entitled, and a cause of that treatment. His diary entry for January 1, 1862, read: "'How do you manage to keep your company so full on drill; asked Agt. Curtis today. Easily. Make the drill cheerfull and pleasant. Dont snarl at them: consider them human." And when his regiment, the Fourth Rhode Island Volunteer Infantry, was shipped on the *Eastern Queen* to Hatteras Inlet, Kent made a special point of caring for his men's needs during the sea voyage. "Some of the Officers stay away from the men too much," he complained. "It is certainly filthy down there and not an agreeable place, but the men can't get out of it and I judge from what I hear now & then among them that they would like to see them often. I make the same number of visits now as when we first came on board and although an unpleasant duty I wont leave it undone."[4]

Lieutenant John S. Wiley had been promoted from the ranks. After a long march in December 1863, he was careful to get his "boys" their ration of whisky. He was proud that he was the first officer in the division to get the ration and prouder of what he overheard. "after I had delt it out to them and turned to come away I could hear the boys say by god that is the man for us he takes some interest in his men it is a pitty thare ant more officers like him in the army." He used the incident to discuss the proper way to command soldiers. "I can command just as much respect from the men by kindness and a great deal more than anyone can by brutal treatment." Consequently, his soldiers were devoted to him; "when I aske one of them to do anything they will jump as if they would brake thare necks to do it." This mutual respect undergird his discipline; having the "good will" of the men, he avoided punishing them. "I dont believe in it—treating men like bruts."[5]

A soldier named David Nichol clearly presented his understanding of what the relationship between officers and men should be within at least the Union army. His assessment was one with which a great many volunteers would have agreed. Nichol was complaining about a new first lieutenant who was too picky and too military for him and his fellow soldiers. The lieutenant's error was his failure to see that volunteer soldiers, differently motivated than soldiers in the regular army, both deserved and required different treatment. The key to this different treatment was the recognition that officers and men were fundamentally equal. "I like to see discipline," Nichol said, "and there can be discipline in the volunteers & still be a good feeling between the officers & men." The regular army, he insisted, could not provide a model, "their Officers follow the army for a Business and the men for a living and of course there will always be a difference between them." But the volunteers acted from far different motives. "In the volunteers we are all enlisted for a certain time and are (or ought to be) actuated by certain motives with a view to the successful termi-

nation of the principles at stake." Given that they were ideologically motivated, "I dont think it necessary to be so strict or
exact or make so wide a difference between Officer & men in
volunteers as regulars just because a man has it in his power to
do so." The different treatment and status of officers and men,
to Nichol and others, were unnecessary for military efficiency,
and it was wrong, practically and morally. "One thing I am
sure of it will not benefit the Cause." Instead of basing his
leadership on rank and military discipline, Nichol insisted
than an officer commanding volunteers needed mutual good
will. "When an Officer has the respect of his men he can lead
them in the hottest of the fight with a clear conscience. can
depend on them to do their duty or all that is required by
him."[6]

Many northern soldiers respected most of their officers
and very much wanted to respect all of them. They preferred
to be led by men whom they could regard as militarily competent and morally above reproach. The fact that their officers
were so often hometown worthies certainly diminished any
awe—already unlikely—that northern soldiers felt for their officers, but it also meant they were men already known and
liked. The ways in which some officers recruited their companies and others were elected by them meant that at the
beginning of the war the average northern officer started with
a reservoir of good will.

The question was how shallow that reservoir would prove
to be. The volunteers of the first half of the war were well
motivated but undisciplined; the more reluctant recruits and
conscripts later were less motivated and far more undisciplined; and even the extremely well-motivated veteran soldiers of the later half of the war were skeptical of officers'
pretensions and unforgiving of military ineptitude which they
knew all too well could get them killed. At no time did the
northern soldier show any particular fondness of having other
soldiers in authority over him. The most vivid example, if not

the most representative, occurred the night that one northern soldier, got drunk, went to his captain's tent, found the captain gone, and decided to urinate all over the tent and then to defecate in the captain's chair.[7]

One problem was that frequently officers had the same amount of military expertise as their men at the beginning of the war—that is to say, none. The average Union officer was not a trained professional. This was not only true in matters of tactics or military discipline—what we tend to think of as "military matters"—but in matters of operating efficiently within the military bureaucracy. The local worthies who raised regiments, the lawyers and businessmen, were products of an economy that could be called pre-corporate, if not pre-industrial. Indeed, in terms of organizing business, the U. S. Army itself vied with the new railroad industry as the leading edge in managerial skills. What most officers had to offer both the organizational and the more narrowly military demands of the Union army was not past experience or training but native intelligence, a willingness to work hard, and literacy. The Union army had a heavy component of men who tried to learn their jobs out of books; fortunately, they soon became men who had learned their jobs out of experience. But until they learned their jobs, it was hard for the soldiers to believe they had particular claims for respect. Sardonic John Crosby said of his officers, "Col Mansfield has tried his best to learn them something of military, so they might be competent to lead men to their death in a s[c]ientific manner." Amos Downing, a soldier in the Sixth Maine, wrote home in October 1861 to complain: "We have been in a considerable danger all ready. Two Co. of our regiment has been within one hundred yard of four South Carolina regt. We might have been all taken prisoner if we had let our officers." Downing argued that the lack of trained officers was the great problem the regiment faced: "we aint got more then two millatary officers." Their colonel was unable to put them "in a line of battle or shift position." "If in case the enemy would attack on the flank we must change position[;] we aint got any officer that kin do it except our Lieut Col." The lieutenant colonel he described as "very smart"; he "understands his business" (a significant phrase). The captain too was a "right smart man," although Downing did not say one way or the other if the captain had any military training. But in general, Downing claimed they had given up on their officers. "We have made up our mind that if the Col leads us in a battle and dont do right, we are determined to fight on our own hook. Our motto is to fire jest as often as we kin and do what we think best."[8]

Sergeant Lucien P. Waters, whose colonel was "a great [schemer] and wirepuller," feared that the soldiers in his regiment would shoot the man if he ever led them into battle: the regiment had not been paid for a while, soldiers' families suffered, and the colonel was to blame. Waters complained that the colonel did not "understand human nature well enough to be popular with the rank and file." "His soldiers are not European machines but freemen who know their rights, and knowing them will have them."[9]

Since the soldiers thought themselves the equals of their officers, they resented any action that seemed to suggest that the officers held themselves superior. Good officers recognized this. We have all seen the photographs of U. S. Grant wearing a plain private's uniform even when he was in command of the entire Union army. Other officers used the same strategy to command. For example, Captain John Pierson shrewdly marched on foot with his company whenever possible. It kept his men more content and encouraged them to greater efforts. He explained that "It is impossible to keep a company together on a march if its commander rides they all want to ride & would not make an effort to keep up but if the Capt marches with his company he has it as hard or harder than any of his men and they will not complain and will keep up as long as they possibly can." What Pierson pointed to was the notion that an officer should lead by setting an example, not simply command. He might had added that the Union soldier rarely felt that their officers were entitled to special privileges such as riding, and that men on horseback underestimated the hardships endured by men on foot.[10]

Testimony from soldiers also suggests that this approach, which appeared egalitarian, worked. One soldier, William P. Patterson, designated his colonel "the best Colenel I have seen yet." His supporting evidence was that unlike other colonels, he rarely rode his horse either on drill and on a march, "he walks when his men walks Caries his haversack and Canteen and runs when his men runs." The colonel explained to his soldiers that he could "stand it as long as his men can." Henry Pippitt praised his captain—"not a beter man in the whole regiment"—because "he would talk with a private just as soon as he would talk with a officer." Another colonel earned this compliment: "A beter man cannot be found to fill that place." But his popularity was with the soldiers, not his fellow officers. "The rest of the officers got down on him because he did not think himselfe enough above the privates, all the privates thought everything of him."[11]

Clearly, not all officers accepted the egalitarian ethos that most soldiers demanded. Some officers seized upon their privileges. A reflective private remembered officers forcing soldiers to get out of the road so they could pass by. He concluded that "the smaller officers who made us jump aside were only following their natural disposition." "You see the same thing in ordinary life," he explained. In civilian life, certain men, if they had more wealth or prestige than their fellows, became "too proud to speak to a former associate." During the war, such men might become officers. "Human nature was the same in the army as out of it. A man who was overbearing and domineering at home was the same way in the army." A less philosophic soldier from Oneida County, New York, characterized the attitudes of his officers toward soldiers thusly: "They *must have*

discipline, and in order to have it the men must know their
places and be made to keep in their places. In fact, they must
learn that they are not men any more." He sneered at the "air"
with which officers "walk through camp and see the men eating bread and coffee (that a dog wouldn't eat in Oneida
County), go to their tents and order a nigger to bring in their
dinner [of] nicely cooked meat and vegetables, then see them
order the men off at double quick to drill or to chop or to dig in
the pits." This soldier—a Democrat commanded by Republican officers—exclaimed in disgust: "These are the men who
are to have the honor of putting down the rebellion and will go
home with a great deal of glory."[12]

Men who felt that their officers received unmerited indul-
gences could go a step farther and believe that these officers
were benefiting from the war; from there they might conclude
that their officers would prefer that the war continue. Christopher Keller, an Illinois soldier, said that "the 'Almighty dollar'
is in the eyes of our Generals and leading men so much that our
country and its interests are almost entirely lost sight of." He
characterized life in the higher ranks as, "Drinking good
brandy, riding sleek horses, flourishing shoulder straps and
bright buttons, and buying cotton to enrich their own
pockets." Why would these men want the war to cease? Keller
said he and his fellow soldiers agreed there was only one way to
end "this miserable war—this wholescale butchery of men."
"They say cut down the pay of every officer to that of the
private and the war will close in less than three months." The
officers, deprived of their comforts, would presumably pros-
ecute the war more vigorously or agree to a negotiated peace.
This, of course, had been the argument of the common soldier
for eons. In *All Quiet on the Western Front,* it is given expres-
sion in the rhyme, "Give them all the same grub and all the
same pay / And the war would be over and done in a day."[13]

Reynolds Griffin, a corporal in the 75th New York Volunteer Infantry, argued that the behavior of their officers dete-

riorated in the course of the war—because of their access to luxury. "They now get drunk, loll around on spring beds that belong to some rich planter and live better than they ever did at home." The exaltation of the officer matched the degradation of the common soldier: "We are degraded nex to the brute, can wallow around in the mud, nasty as hogs, and half starved, and if we chance to complain, they will mention the *guardhouse* to us." Griffin thought that overbearing discipline was no fit treatment for patriotic volunteers. His conclusion was Keller's: "We are simply tools in the hands of the few for the purpose of making money; had it not been for the 'Almighty dollar' this cursed war might have ended long ago."[14]

Before the war, James A. Garfield was an educator; after it he became President. During the war, however, he served as an Union officer. Garfield worried that the habit of command created in officers, particularly those who had made a career of the army before the rebellion, not only an aristocratic spirit, but a pro-slavery attitude. "A command in the army is a sort of tyranny and in a narrow and ignoble mind engenders a despotic spirit, which makes him sympathize with slavery and slaveholders." In his judgment, the military experience was having the opposite effect on the Union volunteer soldiers; "I find the rank and file of the army steadily and surely become imbued with sympathy of slaves and hatred for slavery." Why? "There is at the same time in the position of a soldier in the ranks that which makes him feel the abridgement of liberty and the power of tyranny."[15]

Garfield tended to think of his own responsibilities as an officer in paternal terms. Advising his wife on child-rearing, he asked, "Have you established such a relation between yourself and her as will lay the basis of both strong control and equally strong affection?" These were goals he had commanding soldiers, although he confessed, "Your task with her is harder than mine with the brigade." In fact, Garfield had discovered difficulties in applying his model of paternal command to his

men. In October 1861, he felt "a wider gulf between me and
the men." He had been proud of them, and willing to maintain
"they were not engaged in any irregularities like breaking
guard, etc." He found out he was wrong, and spent a night
hunting troublemakers and arresting them. "It has touched
my pride [and] roused all my determination, till I now feel that
I must be the scourge of many rather than the cooperant friend
and leader." The reciprocal affection he had sought was denied
him; consequently, he had to choose a harsher authority. But
he would have preferred to have acted like a father.[16]

A lot of "the boys" were comfortable with the notion of a
father in authority. Lincoln became for many the great father
figure of the war. "For the last two years of the war especially,
the men had come to regard Mr. Lincoln with sentiments of
veneration and love," Leander Stillwell remembered. "To
them he really was 'Father Abraham,' with all that the term
implied." Of course, many soldiers were young men, used to
paternal authority and their officers—even ones in their late
thirties—seemed to them "old men." Beyond that, given that
orders would be issued and commands obeyed in the army,
some soldiers instinctively preferred a familial model of authority. Henry H. Eby remembered with approval U. S. Grant
disciplining two soldiers: "He talked to them as a father would
to his son." If these paternal accents made soldiers sound like
children, at least they did not make them sound like slaves or
an inferior class or the dregs of society. If a soldier had to
submit to authority, better it be one based on respect and
affection. One of the highest compliments a soldier could pay
an officer was to say he was "like a father" to his men.[17]

When the colonel of the Twentieth Massachusetts died,
the regiment wrote a tribute to him—one guesses that the
actual writing was done by one of the officers. This tribute
contained an abstract disquisition on proper military discipline, the sort that the colonel had exercised. "His discipline
was severe, but not debasing; manly sentiments were encour-

aged, not repressed," the tribute explained. The discipline inculcated self-respect, even in soldiers who had had none previously—the same type of discipline that Captain James Wren, for example, had used to reform Dye Davis. Furthermore, the colonel's discipline, so the tribute claimed, taught a philosophy of authority and obedience to the men in the regiment. "It was demonstrated that discipline should be essential, not merely formal; that obedience, correctness, and zeal were qualities not of external and superficial value alone for the improvement of the machinery of the service but that the man himself was to be benefitted by their observance; that it was for his own advantage and to his own credit that discipline was to be exercised; that the fear of punishment was a low motive only to be appealed to when higher motives failed; but if they failed, the alternative, ignoble and disgraceful as it was, would be inevitable."

Having praised the colonel's discipline, which possessed the power to change soldiers' characters and educate their minds while making the regiment an efficient military unit, the tribute continued expounding a philosophy of discipline. "Military discipline involves submission on the part of inferior, and authority on that of superior," it said. "Any other than such relations are incompatible with the fact, and the idea of discipline." What distinguished true discipline from its sham was law. "While the forms remain the same, obedience may in conscious opposition to law, be rendered from fear, or exacted by force." Obedience to lawless authority—like the obedience of a slave to his master—was "destructive of individuality in the man." And the lawless authority was "tyrannical and unchristian." Proper "obedience should be rendered by voluntary self sacrifice to the law, and authority exercised with equal abnegation of self." When this was the case, as it was with the late colonel's authority, discipline was "ennobling, loyal, and christian."

This was a prescription for an "improving" discipline, an

attempt to render authority acceptable to nineteenth-century Americans. It leans more heavily on notions of character and manhood than it does on the democratic ethos. The good soldier, under the tutelage of his superiors, would become not just an effective soldier—a cog in the "machinery of service"—but a good man. He would learn self-respect and to respect the law. Officers, meanwhile, must recognize that their authority, while necessary to military discipline, must operate in accordance to law. As a defense of authority and obedience, however, this discussion goes beyond the submission of the soldier to military discipline. It could be equally well applied to the relation of the citizen to lawful government. To northern thinking, these precepts, if understood and embraced by all Americans, would have prevented secession. The rebels should voluntarily submit to the rule of law—but since they refused, like the soldier, their obedience must be obtained by force. Furthermore, Confederates could not plead obedience to authority in extenuation of their rebellion: the Confederate government was not a lawful government, and obedience to it was slavish, not manly. Thus military discipline becomes a trope for citizenship and a solution for disunion. As for the colonel who had exercised this exemplary authority, he was described, inevitably, as looking after his men "with the gentleness of a father."[18]

4

*"Mysterious Race of
Grown Up Children"*

COLONEL Thomas Wentworth Higginson, also of Massachusetts, would have agreed with the philosophy of discipline expressed by the resolutions of the Twentieth Massachusetts. He had also considered the relationship between military discipline and men's character. "One half of military duty lies in obedience, the other half in self-respect," he announced. "A soldier without self-respect is useless." This officer also thought carefully about the relationship between soldiers and their commanders and he too had arrived at paternalistic conclusions. "It seems to be the theory of all military usages, in fact, that soldiers are to be treated like children." These conclusions had general applicability. Colonel Higginson developed his philosophy, however, by commanding the First South Carolina Volunteers; he recorded this experience and his philosophy both in his 1869 book *Army Life in a Black Regiment*. Colonel Higginson was a white man who commanded black men.[1]

Higginson was amazing. Born in 1823, he practically grew up at Harvard College, where his father was bursar. He graduated from the college in 1841 and returned later to Harvard's divinity school to become a Unitarian minister—a faith remarkably at odds with that of the southern black men he commanded. He worked as a minister in Newburyport, until his anti-slavery preaching led to his dismissal. Later the Free Church in Worcester welcomed him for much the same reasons that Newburyport had dismissed him. Higginson advocated reform; he was a feminist and an abolitionist. He served on the Boston Anti-Slavery Vigilance Committee, and received a wound on the face during the attempt to rescue the fugitive slave Anthony Burns in May 1854. During 1856 he worked for the Free Soil cause in Bleeding Kansas; in 1859 he was one of the "Secret Six" who financially supported John Brown—and the only one of the six who neither denied knowledge of Brown nor fled the country after the bloody failure at Harper's Ferry. Then, in 1860, Higginson began to prepare in earnest for war with the slavocracy. He read books; he learned fencing and military drill; then he began teaching the drill to Massachusetts volunteers. He was a captain in a Massachusetts regiment when General Rufus Saxton offered the militant abolitionist command of the First South Carolina Volunteers. "I had been an abolitionist too long," he remembered, "and had known and loved John Brown too well, not to feel a thrill of joy at last on finding myself in the position where he only wished to be."[2]

His initial impression of his soldiers was that "all looked as thoroughly black as the most faithful philanthropist could desire; there did not seem to be so much as a mulatto among them." He confessed that "their faces looked impenetrable." In a few days he realized "that some companies, too, look darker than others, though all are purer African than I expected." He learned that Florida soldiers, as compared with the South Carolinians, "average lighter in complexion"—and therefore, to his and probably other white eyes, "look more intelligent."

This reaction in favor of lighter skin—even skin whose comparative lightness he overlooked, dumbfounded instead by the darkness of his soldiers—simply reveals Higginson as a offspring of white American culture. (Indeed, if Higginson did not represent both a strain of northern culture and the restraints that that culture placed around even a sincere reformer, it would be pointless to consider him at such length within the context of this book.) What is more remarkable is how often he argued against the notion that mixed racial ancestry made mulattos superior to people of pure African origins. For example, the two soldiers whom he praised most highly, Prince Rivers, the color sergeant, and Corporal Robert Sutton, he described respectively, as "jet-black, or rather, I should say, *wine-black,*" and "as black as our good-looking Color Sergeant."[3]

"They seem the world's perpetual children, docile, gay, and lovable," Higginson announced—although he modified the characterization by adding "in the midst of this war for freedom on which they have intelligently entered." He told of a sham fight arranged between two companies—"the two companies playing like boys"—which his arrival broke up, and how they asked, "Cunnel, Sah, you hab no objection to we playin', Sah?" They took to military drill faster than white soldiers: "To learn the drill, one does not want a set of college professors; one wants a squad of eager, active, pliant schoolboys; and the more childlike these pupils are the better." When campaigning, he said they took "a childlike pleasure" in getting up early. Even in battle, he thought his soldiers boyish. In one engagement, the Confederates shelled the Union troops—the first time Higginson and his men had been seriously shelled. When the men, initially frightened as most soldiers were by their first experience of shelling, realized that artillery fire was relatively harmless, they relaxed. "They shouted with childish delight over every explosion."[4]

Higginson pushed his analysis beyond the men he commanded. The characteristics he perceived in them could be
explained more than one way. They might be the products of
slavery or of southern culture, and indeed Higginson was always at pains to distinguish between southern black men and
northern black men, apparently preferring the former. (He
had feared that he would find in his soldiers "that sort of
upstart conceit which is sometimes offensive among free negroes at the North, the dandy-barber strut," and was relieved
that the freed people were clear of this.) By one interpretation,
slavery had created dependency in those enslaved, while denying them the opportunity to plan for their futures. Thus they
could not become truly adult. At times Higginson leaned toward this interpretation. But at other times, Higginson invoked racial explanations to explain the characteristics he
found in his soldiers. "Camp life was a wonderfully strange
sensation to almost all volunteer officers, and mine lay among
eight hundred men suddenly transformed from slaves to soldiers," he observed, thus suggesting that the experience of
slavery was what set his soldiers apart. He went on, however,
to say these black soldiers were of "a race affectionate, enthusi-
astic, grotesque, and dramatic beyond all others." Later, intro-
ducing a discussion of African-American religion, Higginson
referred to "this mysterious race of grown-up children with
whom my lot is cast."[5]

Higginson went so far as to argue that black people were
physiologically immature. He believed that white people were
healthier than black ones. Black people lacked the "toughness"
of "the more materialistic Anglo-Saxon." Even though he enjoyed watching active black people, particularly when they
were swimming—"such splendid muscular development, set
off by that smooth coating of adipose tissue which makes them,
like the South-Sea Islanders, appear even more muscular than
they are"—he concluded that they were generally inferior
physically to white people. "Still my conviction of the physical

superiority of more highly civilized races is strengthened on the whole, not weakened, by observing them." They were like children, Higginson said, "easily made ill,—and easily cured, if promptly treated: childish organizations again." He admitted that black soldiers ate poorer rations, did more manual labor, and received less skilled medical treatment than their white counterparts—all of which contributed to health problems. But even so he cited the issue of medical treatment to argue for their essential childishness: "Their childlike constitutions peculiarly needed prompt and efficient surgical care."[6]

Higginson also employed another domestic metaphor to discuss black soldiers. While discussing African-American religion, he observed that it "influences them both on the negative and the positive side." The positive virtues religion gave these men were "zeal, energy, daring." The negative virtues it instilled were what Higginson called "the feminine virtues." Religion made them "patient, meek, resigned." "Imbued from childhood with the habit of submission, drinking in through every pore that other-world trust which is the one spirit of their songs, they can endure everything." Finding that they had "zeal, energy, daring"—presumably masculine virtues—was a relief to the colonel. That the colonel should detect feminine virtues in black men should surprise nobody. American culture had long contrasted both femininity and blackness with "true manhood." And both women and black people were held to remain immature compared with true—white—men.[7]

As he himself acknowledged, Thomas Wentworth Higginson was hardly a demonstrative man. "I have not the reputation of being of an excitable temperament, but the contrary." Evaluating his soldiers, he worked with a definition of manhood in which lack of demonstrativeness was itself a prerequisite of being a true man. This only meant that he shared the general northern understanding of manhood, which invoked the ideal of self-restraint. It was the emotional expressiveness of his soldiers that made him term them childish. They shouted, cried, laughed, played. Of course, white Americans had long maintained the childishness of black people; it was part of what George Fredrickson has called "the black image in the white mind." When Higginson came to South Carolina and found black soldiers enjoying this emotional freedom, he was prepared to identify them as boyish.[8]

And if they were boys, he acted as if he was their father. "Philoprogenitiveness is an important organ for an officer of colored troops; and I happen to be well provided with it." Philoprogenitiveness, for those unfamiliar with the word, refers to love of one's offspring. As noted earlier, Higginson believed that in general "soldiers are to be treated like children." As axiomatic as this was, he thought it even more desirable when commanding southern black soldiers; "these singular persons, who never know their own age till they are past middle life, and then choose a birthday with such precision,— 'Fifty years old, Sah, de fus' last April'—prolong the privilege of childhood."[9]

As a commander, Higginson employed this paternal model of authority. He had ordered a change in officers in one of the companies; the men of the company sent a delegation requesting that at least one of the familiar officers be retained. "Argument was useless; and I could only fall back on the general theory, that I knew what was best for them; which had much more effect." This was of course a favored theory of officers dealing with soldiers, white people dealing with black people, and parents dealing with children. Higginson also reminded them that he had ordered a similar change in another company to that company's benefit. The delegation stayed until Higginson promised that the new company commander would not be "savage to we." The next day, hearing singing in the streets of that company, he reflected that "their griefs may be dispelled, like those of children, merely by permission to utter them." Higginson failed to understand why these freed-

men turned soldiers might seek reassurances about their officers or to consider the discussion between these soldiers and
himself as among men instead of between a father and his
children.[10]

Higginson used paternalism—or its absence—to deny the
legitimacy of slavery. White southerners had claimed that slavery produced an affectionate relationship between masters and
those enslaved. His experience with the First South Carolina
convinced Higginson differently. "I expected to find a good
deal of the patriarchal feeling. It always seemed to me a very ill-
applied emotion, as connected with the facts and laws of
American slavery,—still, I expected to find it." He was looking
for this feeling not in the masters but in those who had been
enslaved; he found "not a particle." "I never heard one speak of
the masters except as natural enemies." This was not, Higginson pointed out, because all masters were cruel or because they
could not distinguish between a kind master and a vicious one.
To the contrary, "some expressed great gratitude to them for
particular favors received." But a kind master was insufficient
to justify the system or to create much patriarchal feeling. "It
was not the individuals, but the ownership of which they complained. That they saw to be a wrong which no special kindnesses could right." Hence the lack of affection for the masters.
Higginson also emphasized that his soldiers seemed motivated
by no desire for revenge against particular masters either—in
fact, he was amazed by their self-control. But the lack of affection surprised Higginson—or so he claimed. He reasoned that
it "did not proceed from any want of personal affection, for
they were the most affectionate people among whom I had ever
lived." They loved, he believed, the good white officers and
even some of the poor ones; they loved him. If they did not love
their masters, "it proved the wrongfulness of the mastery."
Although Higginson would never have granted that the existence of "patriarchal feeling" justified slavery, its absence con-

demned the system. True feelings of affection were to be found not between slave and master but between black soldier and white officer.[11]

Like a good father, Higginson wanted his children to grow up—although, like many a good father, he also sometimes wished his children would never change. In December 1862 he confessed that their "childlike confidence" in him and the other white officers made commanding black soldiers easier. "Nevertheless, it is our business to educate them to manhood." A little over a year later, Higginson wrote that "in every way I see the gradual change in them, sometimes with a sigh, as parents watch their children growing up and miss the droll speeches and confiding ignorance of childhood." The soldiers were becoming "more like white men,—less naive and less grotesque." This acculturation was desirable, no doubt, but nonetheless he regretted it. He hoped that "their joyous buoyancy, at least, will hold out while life does."[12]

Now, it must be remembered that Higginson was drawn to the paternal model of authority in any case. If he cast black soldiers as immature, he also tended to cast white soldiers that way. The first time that the First South Carolina served with white regiments, the Sixth Connecticut and the Eighth Maine, Higginson worried that racial violence might occur within the ranks. He expressed his fears by saying, "if the black and white babies do not quarrel and pull hair, we shall do very well." He cheerfully professed to believe that all soldiers must be treated like children. Perhaps this attitude prevented Higginson from recognizing that his delighted anecdotes of childish freedpeople undercut his principal design in writing *Army Life in a Black Regiment:* generating support among northern white people of political and civil equality for black people.[13]

Colonel Higginson wrote as if most northerners had accepted black manhood, as if the experience of black soldiering, in which he himself had participated, had persuaded white

Americans of the justice of black equality. "It was their de-
meanor under arms," he proclaimed, "that shamed the nation
into recognizing them as men."[14] His initial pleasure that the
soldiers of the First South Carolina were "as thoroughly black
as the most faithful philanthropist could desire" came from his
plans for the regiment: it was to demonstrate the capacity of
black people for freedom. Black initiative had too often been
attributed to mixed ancestry; mulattoes had too often been
held the leaders of the race. If the war along the coast was to be
the proving ground of African Americans, Higginson preferred that the First South Carolina Volunteers rank and file be
"pure African." In 1869, Higginson pointed with pride to the
recent political service of former soldiers. He had already said
of Prince Rivers that "if there should ever be a black monarchy
in South Carolina, he will be its king." After the war, Rivers
and two other sergeants participated in the South Carolina
Constitutional Convention; he and Sergeant Henry Hayne became state legislators. Higginson quoted with approval General Saxton's characterization of black soldiers: "Intensely human."[15]

At the conclusion of *Army Life in a Black Regiment,* Higginson contradicted himself. After portraying the soldiers that
served with him as boys, Higginson next recounted tales of
suffering, endurance, and resistance intended to demonstrate
the adulthood of the freed people. Before serving with the
regiment, the Wilson brothers successfully led their family to
the Union lines and freedom even though all of them were
wounded by gunfire during the escape. It was the grand-
mother in the Miller family who conducted her children and
grandchildren to safety and freedom; the Miller brothers
joined the regiment. Fanny Wright had her baby "shot dead in
her arms" as she crossed from the mainland to an army-
occupied island. Indeed, Higginson suggested here that the
soldiers in the regiment and their families were more adult
than the white junior officers.[16]

One of those officers said of Higginson, "he met a slave and made him a man." But Thomas Long, a private in the regiment, explained matters differently in a sermon during the war. "We can remember, when we fust enlisted, it was hardly safe for we to pass by de camps to Beaufort and back, lest we went in a mob and carried sidearms. But we whipped down all that"—the "all that" was the racist violence of white soldiers—"not by going into de white camps for whip um; we didn't tote our bayonets for whip um; but we lived it down by our naturally manhood; and now de white sojers takes us by de hand and say Broder Sojer. Dats what dis regiment did for de Epiopian race." That was one meaning of black military service; Long continued to explain another one. "If we hadn't become sojers, all might have gone back as it was before; our freedom might have slipped through de two houses of Congress and President Linkum's four years might have passed by and notin' been done for us. But now tings can neber go back, because we have showed our energy and our courage and our naturally manhood." Thomas Long and other soldiers in the First South Carolina insisted that they were already men. He explicated the relationship between manhood, soldiering, and the family in ways that would have easily been understood by a northern volunteer—an image of fathers and children, but not one of paternalistic officers and childish soldiers. "Anoder ting is, suppose you had kept your freedom witout enlisting in dis army, your chilen might have grown up free and been well-cultivated so as to be equal to any business, but it would have been always flung in dere faces—'Your father never fought for he own freedom'—and what could dey answer? Neber can say that to dis African race any more." This dignity was the fruit of the "naturally manhood" of these black soldiers.[17]

And this was the dignity that Higginson ultimately expected white Americans to recognize in black ones. Black military service had proved the right of black men to citizenship—its memory must be perpetuated. Nonetheless, even as he attempted to do this, Higginson also perpetuated old racist stereotypes. What image of black Americans that white Americans would take from reading *Army Life in a Black Regiment* depended on which stories struck them the most—or perhaps on which stories confirmed their prejudices. The image of white parents managing black children was so powerful that Higginson could not escape it, either in structuring his book or in structuring his own experience. The model of parental authority made sense of Higginson's role as colonel of a black regiment. He refused to relinquish this model even when attempting to sustain the ideal of black citizenship.

Higginson was not alone in cherishing this model of race relations. Other white officers commanding black soldiers in the United States Colored Troops shared his understanding. Brigadier General Daniel Ullmann, advising his officers to *"Let the law of kindness be your guide,"* described black soldiers as "docile, impressionable, fully imbued with the spirit of subordination (one of the highest attributes of a soldier), possessed of a deep appreciation of kindly treatment and of keen perceptions, which enables them quickly to discover any flaw in the conduct of their superiors." Even Captain Luis F. Emilio, in his remarkably uncondescending history of the 54th Massachusetts, observed of the soldiers that served with him, "Passive obedience—a race trait—characterized them." Like Higginson, Emilio evoked the paternalistic model of military authority—but like Higginson he would have it applied to all soldiers. "To the soldier his true commander is a father; his superiors, elder brothers to be obeyed; the recruits, his younger kinsmen whom he cares for and supports by example." Chaplain Samuel L. Gardner, who wrote to protest the mistreatment of black soldiers by their white officers, explained such abuses were particularly damaging because the soldiers were "in a state of pupillage." "For my own part, I came into the service under a deep conviction, as a citizen—to speak of

no higher obligation—of the heavy responsibility our government assumed in becoming the guardian of these millions of
freedmen, and from a desire to contribute my help as one man,
toward the great work of leading them up from their enforced
degradation to manhood and citizenship, and I recognize the
military service, in its legitimate operation, as an excellent
school for this end." But such views were shared by some
black officers as well. B. F. Randolph, a black chaplain,
wanted profanity on the part of white officers to cease because
it was a bad example for black soldiers: "The poor oppressed
negro of this land needs the most wholesome example set before him to elevate him."[18]

At the same time, Thomas Long and his fellows in the
First South Carolina were not the only black soldiers who
preferred to think of themselves as men already. In the intro-
ductory essay of their collection of documents on "the black
military experience," Ira Berlin, Joseph P. Reidy, and Leslie
S. Rowland discuss "the well-meaning paternalism of abolitionist officers," arguing that some black soldiers found it
"more distasteful than the simple contempt of racist commanders." They conclude that "black soldiers resented being
treated like children no less than being treated like slaves."
This may be hyperbole, since "being treated like slaves" meant
physical abuse. One of the worst riots of black soldiers occurred in Louisiana in December 1863. Outraged by Lt. Col.
August W. Benedict's whipping of two drummer boys, many
soldiers grabbed their guns, began firing them in the air, and
threatened Benedict alone among the white officers—although
Colonel Charles W. Drew heard one voice cry out, "Kill all the
damned Yankees." Whipping, both here and throughout the
war, reminded black soldiers too forcibly of slavery. But they
also insisted that they knew officers had been ordered not to
strike their men, and they demanded "We want to be treated as
soldiers." Other mutinies conducted by black soldiers also

demonstrated that, just as most white soldiers did, black soldiers rejected the notion that their officers always knew best—i.e., they rejected parental authority.[19]

When the rioters of December 1863 justified their actions by claiming that they had been promised they would not be whipped, they understood their military service as ordered by a contract made among equals. Most of the other mutinies also hinged on the perception that the army and the government failed to keep their end of a bargain, the bargain usually being that of equal pay for white and black soldiers. Higginson himself condemned the government for cheating black soldiers, and helped publicize the demand for equal pay. He pitied the leader of the mutiny in the Third South Carolina, Sergeant William Walker, who "was shot, by order of court-martial, for leading his company to stack arms before their captain's tent, on the avowed ground that they were released from duty by the refusal of the Government to fulfill its share of the contract." As commander of the First South Carolina, Higginson worried that the officers might yet have to execute more soldiers "who, like Sergeant Walker, refuse to fulfill their share of a contract where the Government has openly repudiated the other share." During the battle for equal pay, Higginson recognized the contractual understanding that the soldiers of the First South Carolina had of their enlistments; he also believed that it was only "their childlike faith in their officers" that kept them from mutiny.[20]

Although few spoke with Higginson's seeming authority, some white northerners outside of the black regiments shared his perceptions. Mrs. C. E. McKay, who worked in Union hospitals, visited a contraband camp immediately after the war. "Here are now collected five or six hundred of the colored people, just escaped from the 'barbarism of slavery,'" she said—Higginson once called his black soldiers "young barbarians." Mrs. McKay observed that the freed people "being, as one may say, in the infancy of manhood, the Government, like a 'cherishing mother,' is holding them by the hand until they shall be able to go alone."[21]

The familial model of race relations was hardly the only one available to white northerners, not even the only racist model. One guesses that it was a model that particularly attracted those who felt kindly toward African-Americans. While condescending toward those people, it at least asserted mutual bonds between white and black, and encouraged a sense that white people had some sort of responsibility toward black people. Other white Americans would have disagreed. Most anti-black sentiment was much harsher in tone; according to other white Americans, including many northern soldiers, black people were more savage than childish. White people, it was believed, owed black people nothing. And when the government did propose aid to the freed people, it was viewed in much the way Mrs. McKay viewed it as she watched them in the contraband camp—a paternal government holding the hands of black children.

The hierarchal relationship of white people to black people in the Union army reinforced paternalism among northerners as well as reflected it. Segregation structured the military experience so that white soldiers did not develop camaraderie with black soldiers within their messes, companies, and regiments. White men in black regiments were officers commanding their "boys." White and black men were rarely fellow soldiers. They might fight side-by-side in battle but they belonged to different companies—which was to say different families, different communities. Black soldiering could change white men's image of black men, but it created fewer reciprocal bonds than it might have. Despite the paternalistic constructs of men like Higginson, few northerners embraced black men as either "sons" or "brothers." The image of the family remained white only. Perhaps this was one reason, among so many, that during the years of sectional reconciliation, the nation managed to forget the contribution black people made to the salvation of the Union.

There is a famous image of Thomas Wentworth Higginson that dates from the period of reconciliation. Reading "Marse Chan," Higginson wept. Thomas Nelson Page's story is a tale of a black slave's loyalty to his young master, a slaveholder and a Confederate. Higginson's response to the tale seemed odd indeed, for he had a long anti-slavery career and he had denied the existence of affection of slaves for masters. Edmund Wilson argued that the northern approval of Thomas Nelson Page's fiction came from "feelings of guilt" about the war, and suggested that Higginson may have shared these feelings. Perhaps—although Higginson never lost interest in black rights the way so many other white northerners did. Given Higginson's paternalistic ideals, perhaps there is less of a contradiction between his life and the way "Marse Chan" brought tears into his eyes than there initially seems. He wanted his black soldiers to love him the same way.[22]

5

Men Without Women: The Need for Femininity in a Masculine World

IN spring 1864, before the season's campaigning began, Massachusetts troops stationed at Brandy Station, Virginia, amused themselves by holding balls. They wanted more than simply an occasion to dance; they wanted to reproduce the experience of a ball back home as much as possible. But could they really have a ball without women? Instead of relying on local women—rebellious and, even worse, too few in number—for their balls, they created their own. Soldiers, particularly drummer boys, dressed as ladies for the night. At one ball, an estimated sixty men disguised themselves. One soldier wrote home that "some of the real women went but the boy girls was so much better looking they left." He added, "no one could hav told wich of the party had fell on a *hatchet.*" Another soldier agreed: "We had some little Drummer boys dressed up and I'll bet you could not tell them from girls if you did not know them." Indeed, he said, "some of them looked almost good enough to *lay* with and I guess some of them did get layed with"—a reference probably to the fact the soldiers habitually slept in the same quarters and not to some homosexual activity. If it was the latter, then it is surprising he would confess to his wife, "I know I slept with mine."

The best joke was one played on an officer. This major was captivated by a young man who was "the bell of the evening." Fellow soldiers introduced him to the major as a local girl. The major pursued him all evening and finally got him alone in the drawing room. At that point, the soldier pulled up his dress, displayed his privates, and "asked the Major how he liked the looks."[1]

One could use this story in many different ways. It is tempting to see in this some sort of carnival inversion, the ordinary soldiers mocking the ordered world of the army and successfully casting ridicule on their officers. The soldiers certainly found humor in the situation. Yet their motivation seems to have been less burlesque and more nostalgic. They missed their homes; they missed the social entertainments to which they had been accustomed; they missed women. With Yankee ingenuity, then, they improvised a temporary solution to the absence of women by becoming women themselves.

This is the image to keep in view: a society of men, of soldiers, transforming itself for a spell into a sexually mixed society. The importance of this image is that it suggests that to these nineteenth-century northerners there could be no such thing as a purely masculine world. If those who were to bear the feminine values of nurture were absent, then the soldiers themselves had to embody them. This trope touched more aspects of the Union soldiers' experience than just a few hilarious dances held in a dull time the spring of 1864.

Northern culture put domesticity at the center of society and women at the center of domesticity. Yet, like a sailing vessel or a monastery, the army was an exclusively male preserve. This presented a problem for soldiers who wanted their service to be a sign of their good moral conduct. The army was engaged in the virtuous process of crushing rebellion—but without women, its own virtue seemed difficult to maintain. A Connecticut soldier, perhaps accidentally, summed up the way military life violated much of nineteenth-century thinking on the social order. "There is no society here," he complained to his wife, "there is nothing but men."[2]

Northern soldiers frequently sounded desperate for the company of women—and not for sexual companionship alone. Lyman C. Holford complained that, in his remote army camp, "we don't see hardly anyone except men in Uniform and we have got so that we consider them as all belonging to the same family." "It seems as if we were almost out of the world." And S. H. Eels reported home that the "strangest sight out here is to see a *woman.*" When one appeared, the soldiers would cry out, "There's a woman, boys," and the soldiers would hurry to see her, "as if she were some great curiosity." When the wife of an officer at one outpost came to visit her husband, the soldiers crowded the landing to get a glimpse of her. Then, "they formed a lane for her, shouting, throwing up their caps, and acting in such a way generally that the poor woman was frightened and ran as fast as she could to her husband's quarters." When, in John William De Forest's *Miss Ravenel's Conversion from Secession to Loyalty,* the colonel's wife joins her husband, "the whole Brigade knew her, and delighted to look at her, drilling badly in consequence of inattention when she cantered by on horseback." Calling her the Queen of the Lafourche Interior, De Forest noted that the "adulation which she received did not come from the highest human source, but it was unmixed, unshared, whole-hearted, constant." Officers confined in Richmond's Libby Prison would crowd the windows in "wild excitement" to peer at a woman walking down the street. John Wesley Marshall gratefully noted in his diary that "the ringing of church bells sounds with delight upon our ears[;] how home like it seemes to be once more in a place where both sexes are seen going to the place of worship."[3]

Women were key to domesticity and its virtues, key to the homes and community which many soldiers thought their service defended. With femininity so central to good social order, the absence of women could be perceived as a threat. Women provided the moral influence that kept men from temptation and on the path of virtue. Evaluating the way fresh recruits fit into regiments of seasoned veterans, Orra Bailey had to allow to his wife that army life made men "rough." "It no doubt makes men rougher to take them from the restraints of society and of the fair secx. We of course admit that the wimmen have great influence in softenning our rougher natures." But his regiment had been away from the softening influence of women for seventeen months. "Would it be very strange if their should be some very rough fellows amongst us especially among the yonger portion of them?" Men without women had to fear moral degradation—or, as one soldier put it when censuring the laxity of Sabbath observance in the army, "Man's tendency, unrestrained by the purifying influence of woman is downward." Long after the war, Wilbur Fisk explained that "Someone has said that Woman carried civilization in her heart." In the Union army, unfortunately, men had been away from feminine society. Fisk said, "A man that lives in a community where he has the privileges of woman's society becomes more refined than he is aware of but when he is away from that the very best of men will degenerate or at least they will feel the deprivation."[4]

Women were the fount of virtue. Beyond that, domestic ideology identified them as the source of nurture. A true woman provided the solace that men required—made for them a "haven in a heartless world." The man was expected to venture forth into this heartless world, for such was his role, but he was expected to return to the domestic world for healing. Nurture was not separate from woman's role as the source of moral value but integral to it. A good woman nurtured, and her nurture was the means by which boys and men had good moral sense inculcated.[5]

Now, as we have discussed before, the northern soldier did expect to return to his home after the war was done. His military service could be comprehended in terms of domestic ideology. He had left the hearth not just to wrestle a living from the heartless world but to defend his home; once victory was achieved, he would return to that home—provided that he did not instead find his home in heaven. But until then he had to live in the world of the army, the world of war. Yet it was in this world, where he risked his life and endured hardship, that he most needed the nurturing that his culture told him was characteristic of women. The lack of feminine presence meant that the masculine world of the army was incomplete. A society without some feminine leavening was inconceivable. Nurture, kindness, compassion were all the more necessary on the battlefield because they were unlikely. There could be no such thing as a purely masculine world. Something would have to be improvised.

The Union army had a female component literally. Women did accompany the army. Besides the southern women, white and black, that soldiers encountered, there were women who came down from the north. These included visitors to the soldiers—wives, mothers, and other family members—prostitutes, and, most important, nurses and hospital agents. The nurse was the woman who above all others restored some femininity to the lives of men at war. Even though nursing required women to leave their homes—and indeed to challenge some assumptions of male supremacy, nursing could be viewed as an extension of woman's domestic sphere.[6]

The most comfortable role for nurses to seize upon was the maternal one. They presented themselves to the soldiers—

almost always called "the boys"—as mothers. At one time Mary Livermore served aboard a hospital boat on the Mississippi River; when the nurses encountered sick and wounded soldiers, "we fell into maternal relations with them, as women instinctively do when brought into juxtaposition with weakness, and were soon addressing them individually as 'my son,' 'my boy,' or 'my child.' One woman came to nurse her son, but found he had died before her arrival; she stayed, however, to nurse "the sons of other mothers who were far away." Thinking of nursing as mothering made it fit with these women's conceptions of their feminine duties, even though they were acting as mothers to hundreds of surrogate sons.[7]

The maternal role came easily to those women who actually were mothers, particularly mothers of sons the age of the soldiers. But it came also as easily to women who had had no children at all. True, Louisa May Alcott confessed she received the affection of the patients because "I was the poor substitute for mother, wife, or sister," but she seems to have accepted a maternal role. Emily Elizabeth Parsons, an unmarried nurse in her late thirties, referred to her ward of patients as "my children"—sometimes to their faces; one day a patient gave her "such a loving look" that "it made me think of his far off mother." All this even though she had some hopes of gaining a husband through her nursing. Other nurses agreed that their appearance reminded the soldiers of "mother and home."[8]

Another acceptable role was that of "sister"—although I think this was less common. Julia Wheelock, serving chicken broth to a room full of wounded men, was told by one, "Oh, you are so kind, I don't know what to call you, unless it be sister." She answered, "Very well, I'll be your sister." Other nurses actually were Sisters—the Catholic orders contributed heavily to the ranks of nurses.[9]

Besides mother and sister, the remaining roles were sweetheart and wife. These were, of course, too dangerous.

Indeed, Dorothea Dix preferred that her nurses be middle-aged and plain to avoid such dangers—although the real worry came less from the soldiers than from the doctors. (One nurse advised her daughter that the young doctors viewed young nurses as their "natural prey.") Still, the power of the conception of the woman as wife was such that occasionally it surfaced. Emily Parsons, I believe, hoped to find domestic happiness through her nursing; if so, she was disappointed. A widow came to Benton Barracks Hospital, hoping for "consolation in nursing"; another nurse observed, not kindly, "I suppose she thinks fifty men will console her for one." It was more seemly for women to cast themselves as sisters or mothers.[10]

While the nurses themselves may had created the notion that they could substitute for absent mothers, soldiers connived at the confusion too. Reading accounts of men in the hospital reminds us that men in extreme pain and stupefaction, frequently delirious, are prone to revert to a childlike state. Emily Parsons noted that soldiers who had been sick a long while suffered a "weariness"; "The peculiar sort of submissiveness it causes is like that of a poor tired child who wants somebody to take care of him, and is too weak to do for himself." When Mary Livermore was with the Chicago sanitary commission, soldiers from the hospital would come to visit. "They are praised heartily, petted in motherly fashion, as if they were children, which most sick men become." At the battle of Chancellorsville, a nurse administered a stimulant to a badly wounded young officer whose arm had been amputated. He asked her if she came from Philadelphia—"Because you are so kind"—and when she asked, "Do all the kind people live in Philadelphia?" he answered, "No . . . mother." And suffering conveyed other soldiers home, at least in their minds. Livermore observed a teenage soldier "raving in the delirium of brain fever." He was convinced he was not in a military hospital but back at home; he "incessantly appealed" to his mother for "a drink of water right from the spring at the back of the house, the clearest and coldest in all Illinois." One man, shot through the lungs, cried out in his sleep, "Mother! Mother! Mother!" Hannah Ropes got out of bed and went to him, as a mother would to her child. "The pressure of blood from the unequal circulation had affected the brain slightly, and, as they all are, he was on the battlefield, struggling to get away from the enemy." She "promised him that nobody should touch him, and that in a few moments he would be free from all pain." He turned his eyes on her, and she watched him die— "his breathing grew more gentle, ending as softly as an infant's."[11]

Men who were ill might be expected to cry out for mothers, but after they had recovered the soldiers still referred to these women in maternal terms. The role of mother—as compared with a "masculine" role such as doctor—was the role it was easiest for the men to place their nurses in. One fifteen-year soldier suffering from typhoid and depression refused to eat anything unless it was "like mother used to make." Katharine Wormeley, a nurse with the Sanitary Commission, said that the "favorite speech" of any soldier receiving some kindness from her hand was "Oh, that's good; it's just as if mother were here!" Hannah Ropes, who embraced her maternal roles, was nonetheless surprised when "one quite old man," with a bullet hole in his right hand, called her "good mother." A soldier asked a Catholic sister to "write to my mother, and tell her I was cared for in my suffering by a band of ladies who were as tender to me as mothers."[12]

Hannah Ropes also pointed out one simple, even naive, reason for the soldiers' insistence that nurses were mothers. "Wounded men are exposed from head to foot before the nurses and they object to anybody but an 'old mother.'" Pain and illness made men look for their mothers, while embarrassment and enfeeblement made them feel small children once again. But just as important, the range of roles that men associated with "good women"—and these caring ladies were manifestly "good women"—was so narrow they were almost forced to think of them as mothers.[13]

The maternal role, in turn, allowed nurses to claim a maternal authority. Sometimes they found their moral authority—what Mrs. McKay called "woman suasion"—extended beyond the hospital. Mrs. McKay herself was called on to stop a vicious fight between two soldiers. "Without a moment's thought," she recalled, "I ran to the spot where was the humiliating spectacle of two of our men, their faces already bloody and swollen, grappling and fisty-cuffing each other with the fury of wild beasts, while a dozen or more of their comrades, standing around, were urging on the fight." She placed her hand on one of the fighters and "uttered a few words of surprise and shame," and the two soldiers, still grumbling, broke off the fight. Mrs. McKay believed her authority came from her representation of the women back home; she thought "that it was not so much my personal presence as the suggestion of some mother, wife, or sister, far away, that tamed their ferocity, and shamed them out of their bloody purpose."[14]

Hannah Ropes used her political influence to have a hospital steward fired and the doctor in charge of the hospital imprisoned when she decided that they mistreated patients. Challenged by the doctor, once he had been set free, she justified what he called interference by her mother's role. "I am a mother, and I have only to remember that each of these sick ones [has] a mother somewhere, and for the time I act for them." She also based her authority on her own strident reading of nineteenth-century doctrines of womanly moral perfection: "a woman's intuitions, which if she lives an orderly life are as unerring as the finger of God."[15]

The soldiers granted these "mothers" authority out of proportion to their military authority. The delight the soldiers took in them came from their very womanness, their domesticity. When Emily Parsons gave a wounded man a glass of water, another soldier told her, "It is real cheery now, to have a

woman come round one, it seems like home." Hospital agent
Julia S. Wheelock put the same sentiment in more grandiose
phrases. She explained that ladies ministering to the army had
nothing to fear from the soldiers: "Any one, during war's dark
hours, whose mission was to do good, was almost an object of
worship by those wholly excluded from home influences."
Using language that called on Lincoln's first inaugural with
unconscious irony—in 1861 the "better angels" failed to restrain the southern states—she said, "If there ever was a time
when the better angels of their nature guarded the citadel of
their hearts, it was in the presence of woman—when she was a
true representative of what that sacred word implies."[16]

Nurses valued themselves for the way they brought
"home influences" into the sphere of war itself: if soldiers were
dutiful—or even miscreant—sons, the nurses were their com-
passionate mothers. No woman who served as a nurse remained blind to the horrors of the war—occasionally their
clinical accounts of wounds and infections foreshadow Hemingway's grimmest prose—but some of them continued to believe that the presence of a woman alleviated both physical
suffering and psychological anguish. Women imbued with
domestic ideology thought that they were "true representatives" of feminine virtue. Many soldiers responded to these
women and the images they projected just as the women
hoped they might. Like the nurses themselves, soldiers prized
their service as bringing feminine virtue into their harshly
masculine sphere. When Jane Swisshelm tried to comfort one
patient, he cried out, "Oh you will think I am a baby!" She
replied, "Your past life is sufficient certificate of your manhood; and now has come your time to be a baby, while I am
mother."[17]

When Rice C. Bull's "tentmate and friend Spencer" came
down with typhoid fever, he was sent to the hospital. Bull

visited him. Spencer was recovering from his fever, but gangrene had developed in both feet. "He was overjoyed to see me and insisted that I must stay and nurse him." Even though he thought the request unnecessary, Bull consulted with the surgeon—only to learn that Spencer probably would die. "The Surgeon explained that his feet were mortified [gangrenous], that his only hope was to have good care, and this was not available in the hospital at that time." Horrified, Bull went back to his regiment and got his colonel's permission to nurse Spencer. He learned what diet and medicine his friend required, and how to clean the wounds in his feet. Bull bunked in Spencer's ward, which he had learned was the "death ward." "Spencer was glad to see me. He had been in low spirits but said now that I was with him he would have some chance to get well." After two days, the surgeon amputated some of Spencer's toes. Spencer's brother, whom Bull had sent for by telegraph, arrived; Spencer received a furlough to go home; and Bull felt he could return to his regiment. The surgeon asked him to stay on as a nurse, but Bull refused: "Nothing could have induced me to continue in that work. This had been my first experience in the horrors of war as shown by our terrible Hospital Service." The only bright spot in the experience had been "the presence and loving service of an old Quaker woman, the only woman nurse I saw in the place."[18]

Thousands of soldiers entered the hospitals, but many of them failed to encounter true representatives of sacred womanhood. Thousands more never set foot in the hospital or granted to a kindly nurse surrogate motherhood. While some women succeeded in bringing feminine values to some soldiers, most of the army had to get by somehow without virtuous woman. No doubt some—a few—embraced this world of "men without women"—to borrow Ernest Hemingway's phrase. Most longed to return to the heterosocial world. But in order to function in this masculine world, men found that they themselves had to embody some virtues thought feminine. Like the dancers at the 1864 balls, sometimes they had to act like women.

Many feminine aspects of the soldiers' experience were trivial. For example, soldiers found themselves doing chores that had traditionally been considered womanly. Now they were cooking, washing and mending clothes, cleaning their camps. In fact, a sewing kit, such as the two Cyrus Boyd received from two different young ladies, was known as a "housewife." Boyd thought every soldier needed such a housewife. Laforest Dunham apologized for writing a short letter home by explaining, "I have first got my dishes washed and the shantie swept out and I must do some washing today." "What's the use of women anyway?" one soldier asked another. "We cook our own victuals, wash and mend our own clothes, make up our own beds—and what more could women do?" Another soldier wrote his sister, "You also asked me who would Clean my ears sins I am out here." He confessed, "I reckon I haf to do that myself and wash my cloth and Cook my victles and mend my Cloth." Thinking of women's chores— though it's hard to imagine precisely why his sister had been the one to clean his ears before the war—reminded him of the question of women's company in general. "I havent to say the real truth spoken three words to a femail sins I left home." He disliked "secesh women," and they didn't care for Yankees. The one attractive southern woman he had met made "an awful face" at him.[19]

The problem of men without women went beyond worries about chores that men thought unmanly and at which they were embarrassingly inept. There were other duties which were thought particularly suited for women and yet which men at war had to assume. It was the officers—those leaders of men—who most often had to display feminine virtues. For example, they had the feminine responsibility of nurturing their soldiers physically. Officers had to try to keep their soldiers fit, which required them to oversee diet, cleanliness,

Informed by a culture that put home at the center of society, northerners imagined the Union as a family writ large. Thus they could portray sectional conflict as familial strife.

THE OLD MAN AND HIS SONS.

An old Man had many Sons, who were often quarrelling with one another. When the father had exerted his authority, and used other means to reconcile them, but all to no purpose, he at last had recourse to this expedient; he ordered his Sons to be called before him, and a short bundle of sticks to be brought; then commanded them each to try if, with all his might and strength, he could break it. They all tried, but to no purpose; for the sticks being closely and compactly bound up together, it was impossible for the force of man to do it. After this, the father ordered the bundle to be untied, and gave a single stick to each of his Sons, at the same time bidding him try to break it; which when each did with all imaginable ease, the father addressed them to this effect: "O, my Sons, behold the power of unity; for if you, in like manner, would but keep yourselves strictly conjoined in the bonds of friendship, it would not be in the power of any mortal to hurt you; but when once the ties of brotherly affection are dissolved, how soon you become exposed to every injurious hand that assaults you!"

MORAL.—Union is Strength.

Harper's, February 2, 1861.

MAMMA (*born North*). "Dear! dear! dear!—What a pity it is you can't agree!"

SMALL BOY (*born South*). "Well, Mamma, we should agree, only she's so unkind!—She won't be a Pig, and let me drive her about by the Leg!"

Harper's, June 1, 1861.

Northerners saw joining the army to fight for the Union as an extension of a man's duty to protect his family. Reluctance to volunteer was viewed as stemming from a lack of manhood.

Harper's, November 7, 1863.

CLARA.—"Don't you think it an anomaly, Tom, your preparing to fight for your hearth and home, while you have not a wife?"

Harper's, June 27, 1863.

Costume suggested for the Brave STAY-AT-HOME "LIGHT GUARD."

Harper's, September 14, 1861.

WIFE. "He shouldn't go to the horrid war, away from his 'wifey, tifey,' and spoil his pretty mustache, so he shouldn't, sweet little boy. He shall have a petticoat and a broom, and stay at home."

Harper's, August 31, 1861.

If the soldier fought for the Union and his home, the company he joined fought for the Union and his hometown. The companies and regiments sent to war represented the communities of the North.

(Photograph by J. A. Simmonds. The Western Reserve Historical Society, Cleveland, Ohio)

Away from home, soldiers began to feel a new sense of community in their companies. Officers and men tried to strike the proper balance between manly independence and the necessity for discipline. Some saw military discipline as fatherly. Paternalism particularly influenced the way some white officers treated the black soldiers they commanded.

(*U.S. Army Military History Institute*)

HARPER'S WEEKLY.
A JOURNAL OF CIVILIZATION

VOL. VII.—No. 324.]   NEW YORK, SATURDAY, MARCH 14, 1863.   [SINGLE COPIES SIX CENTS.
$4.00 PER YEAR IN ADVANCE.

Entered according to Act of Congress, in the Year 1863, by Harper & Brothers, in the Clerk's Office of the District Court for the Southern District of New York.

TEACHING THE NEGRO RECRUITS THE USE OF THE MINIE RIFLE.—[See Page 174.]

Harper's, March 14, 1863.

The women of the North encouraged patriotism, some bringing the female quality of nurture and compassion into the hospital and camp. Good mothers raised their sons to be loyal. Southern women, however, were viewed as enemies who gloried in rebellion and had lost their true womanly virtues.

AN UNWELCOME RETURN.
THREE MONTHS' VOLUNTEER. "What! don't you know me—your own husband?"
DAUGHTER OF COLUMBIA. "Get away! No husband of mine would be here while the country needs his help."

Harper's, August 10, 1861.

Harper's, August 30, 1862.

SCENE, FIFTH AVENUE.
HE. "Ah! Dearest ADDIE! I've succeeded. I've got a Substitute!"
SHE. "Have you? What a curious coincidence! And I have found one FOR YOU!"

(Chicago Historical Society)

(*U.S. Army Military History Institute*)

THE LADIES OF NEW ORLEANS before GENERAL BUTLER's Proclamation.

Harper's, July 12, 1862.

After GENERAL BUTLER's Proclamation.

Harper's, July 12, 1862.

Harper's, February 7, 1863.

Harper's, June 7, 1862.

Sectional reconciliation could also be presented in familial images. A war to restore the Union demanded the image of the family made whole.

THE RETURN HOME.

COLUMBIA. "Tell me, Soldier, did you not pass a Wayward Sister of mine on the road?"
RETURNING SOLDIER. "I did. I fetched her a good part of the way myself; but she says she don't require my services any more now; and here she comes over the hill."

Harper's, June 1865.

Harper's.

360,000 deaths, however, left many northern families broken. Death itself was thought of as going home, and grief was to be assuaged by patriotic pride, rituals of mourning, and the vision of reunion in the afterlife.

Harper's, November 2, 1861.

(Courtesy, Vermont Historical Society)

(*National Archives*)

Those veterans who returned safely would often explain their wartime service in terms of true manhood, virtuous mothers, and the influence of home.

From *Reminiscences of Three Years' Service in the Civil War by a Cape Cod Boy*, by John J. Ryder, Reynolds Printing, New Bedford, Mass., 1928.

health, and other matters associated with a mother's care. One Ohio soldier reported that his captain had the whole company vaccinated, because he was "bound to do all he can to keep us from getting sick." "He seems to be everywhere, and at the same time stops us from eating greasy food, & c." The captain told his company that, if a soldier came down sick, he would be "welcome to anything this table affords." During the battle of South Mountain, Captain James Wren discovered a pile of Confederate knapsacks containing clean clothes and made the men of his company change their socks, shirts, and underwear; "I had it done in 6 or 8 squads for fear we would be Driven away while undressing & Changing." Officering a company also required that one become a teacher—in an era when teaching increasingly was associated with woman's roles. The officer taught men military drill, military duties, basic sanitation. Sometimes he felt obliged to instruct them in the political issues surrounding the war.[20]

The most important feminine duty learned by officers was consolation. An officer had to learn to talk to his soldiers when they were discouraged and write the letters home that simultaneously announced the death of a loved one and offered comfort to the family. As much of the labor and emotion of consoling the widowed and fatherless as could be was turned over to chaplains; often common soldiers wrote; in the main, however, the job of informing the family of the dead man fell to the company commanders.

By nineteenth-century northern domestic ideology, consolation was a supremely feminine task. An incident that occurred during Louisa May Alcott's hospital service epitomizes this. One patient was clearly dying. The doctor gave Alcott the duty of informing him: "Bless you, there's not the slightest hope for home; and you'd better tell him so before long; women have a way of doing such things comfortably, so I leave it to you." As Ann Douglas observes, in her *Feminization of American Culture,* "The world of consolation literature is a domestic and personal one, a place where the minister and the mother become at last the only genuine authorities."21

But ministers and mothers were not always available. Usually, an officer had to take on their role. Officers, after all, had recruited these men into the companies and led them away from their homes and families. Now announcing, describing, and explaining their deaths to the people they left behind became part of an officer's duty. Hardest of all was trying to console those whose grief often began with the arrival of the very letter of consolation.

On July 10, 1864, Captain David Critchlow, commanding company "C" of the 100th Pennsylvania Veteran Volunteer Regiment, then in the trenches around Petersburg, Virginia, had to write such a letter to the father of Corporal Fred Pettit. Pettit had just returned to his company after a bout in the hospital only to have a sharpshooter kill him. "It becomes my painful duty to inform you that your noble son is no more. He was killed yesterday about seven o'clock P.M., the ball entering the left side of his neck and reaching the surface at the right cheek, producing instant death. He was sitting in his place reading at the time." Fred Pettit may well have been killed instantly—in the trenches, one's head was the most likely target presented—but describing death as instantaneous was a kindly convention of the consolation letter then and later. Nonetheless, the specificity of detail about the wound is surprising—the Pettits could easily envision the course of the bullet through their son's neck and head.

That grim duty over, the captain continued. Now he tried to console Pettit's "afflicted and sorrowing" family. He did so by praising the character of their "noble son." Pettit, he said, "died as he lived, a devoted and exemplary Christian"; "I trust and believe that your loss is his eternal gain." Besides his Christianity, Pettit's family should take pride in his courage and devotion to duty: "As a soldier, Fred was brave and always at his post." Finally, the captain gathered together Pettit's few belongings—a Bible, a testament, a hymnbook, and a diary—and sent them home.

This was the condolence letter stripped down to its components. In a few lines, Critchlow invoked most of the major themes—Pettit was a "noble son," a Christian whose soul was now in heaven, and a good soldier. Critchlow only missed describing Pettit's death as a patriotic sacrifice and remarking on his devotion to his family. Pettit was one of the twenty-eight officers and soldiers of company "C" who were killed during the Civil War. I do not know if Capt. Critchlow wrote twenty-seven more consolation letters.

But he was not the only one to write Fred Pettit's family a letter of consolation. C. P. Critchlow—the captain's wife—also accepted that duty: "I received a letter from Mr. Critchlow on Saturday giving me the sad news of your son Fred's death." She repeated details which the captain had given her, and expressed her "heartfelt sympathy." Then her own anxiety and fear caused her to add a sentence. "I feel as though any day may bring me sorrowful tidings as they are hourly exposed to the guns of the enemy." Her sympathy was heartfelt, because she already imagined receiving news of her husband's death. Because of delays in the mail, it was Mrs. Critchlow's letter, not Capt. Critchlow's, that informed the family of Fred Pettit's death.[22]

Even Abraham Lincoln tried his hand at writing a consolation letter, employing those same cadences we know so well from the Gettysburg Address to comfort one mother on the death of all her sons. Massachusetts Governor John Andrew approached Lincoln about Mrs. Lydia A. Bixby, a Boston widow. Applying for governmental assistance, she said all five of her sons had died in battle. The governor wanted Lincoln to write her a letter, very much the same kind of letter that Lincoln's captains had learned to write to other grieving mothers.

Lincoln too started with the fact of death. "I have been shown in the files of the War Department a statement of the

Adjutant-General of Massachusetts that you are the mother of five sons who have died gloriously on the field of battle." Then, with the feelings of inadequacy that bothered most people who confronted those mourning, he tried to console her. "I feel how weak and fruitless must be any words of mine which should attempt to beguile you from the grief of a loss so overwhelming. But I cannot refrain from tendering you the consolation that may be found in the thanks of the Republic they died to save." After assuring her of the nation's thanks, he offered her, as far as he could, God's blessing. "I pray that our heavenly Father may assuage the anguish of your bereavement, and leave you only the cherished memory of the loved and lost, and the solemn pride that must be yours to have laid so costly a sacrifice upon the altar of freedom." As one who lost his own son during his presidency, Abraham Lincoln was well acquainted with loss and mourning and the hope that only cherished memories would be left.

As for Lydia Bixby, the letter gave her a kind of fame. But she had deliberately or unknowingly deceived the Massachusetts authorities. Two of her sons had been killed. One had been captured but had also been exchanged. The fourth had deserted the Union army and gone to sea. A fifth, having been captured, had enlisted in the Confederate army. Mrs. Bixby hadn't particularly been seeking a presidential consolation letter anyway; she wanted money to live on. None of this really lessens her grief. But the spectacle of her misleading the authorities and raising at least two sons of dubious patriotism, undercut the very notions of feminine moral influence.[23]

Indeed, the Civil War created another problem for the belief in the moral superiority of women. What about all those rebels in the South? Didn't they have mothers too? And if they were rebellious, hadn't the women of the South, those responsible for inculcating patriotism, failed in their duty to the country? If womanly nurture made men what they were, southern women bore culpability for the rebellion.

So, at the same time that the war raised the worth of some women—the virtuous mothers, sisters, and wives of the North—in the eyes of Union soldiers, it lowered the worth of other women, such as prostitutes and particularly the "secesh she-devils" of the South. A woman's success in her domestic duties could be measured politically: which side did her sons take in the war for the Union? And beyond that test, there were those exceptional women who actually brought feminine virtues to the front, by serving as nurses or in other capacities. Did they leave their homes—or did they extend the home? On the one hand, they participated in the war directly, not simply through the sacrifice of their sons; on the other hand, their service was perceived as essentially maternal. They both challenged and confirmed American notions of true womanhood and of separate spheres.

In the immediate experience of the war as lived in the army, what became valued most were those men who could impersonate the feminine values of nurture and compassion. No wonder Lincoln became the northern soldiers' greatest hero, for they imagined him to embody both femininity and masculinity, the mother and the father, most perfectly. For a man's feminine virtues to be esteemed, he had to affirm the masculine virtues as well. In that odd sense, the Civil War pointed toward creating a complete human personality. Ann Douglas and others have shown how the pursuit of their feminine natures in nursing required women to assume masculine values of assertion and authority. The preeminent masculine pursuit of war forced men to develop some of the feminine virtues within themselves. "Men without women" had to learn at least some of the virtues they had regulated to the domestic sphere.

6

She Devils

"The venom of the she adder is as dangerous as that of the
he adder."

*Aphorism said to have been displayed in the New
Orleans office of General Benjamin F. Butler.*

DURING the burning of Columbia, South Carolina, the
Union provost marshal, perhaps feeling guilt because he could
not protect the city, told a bitterly complaining woman, "The
women of the South kept the war alive—and it is only by
making them suffer we can subdue the men." When the
mayor's wife provoked another soldier, announcing that she
wished she had more sons to give to the Confederate army, he
taunted her, saying, "damn you women, you are the ones keeping up the war." And after the fire, when Columbia women
asked W. T. Sherman to protect them, he asked "Where are
your fathers and husbands and sons? Why are they not here to
protect you?"[1]

* * *

The women that the soldiers encountered did not always live up to the requirements of true womanhood. If the North sent the soldiers motherly nurses, it also contributed prostitutes to the war effort. In spring 1863, one northern soldier encountered a prostitute in Fredericksburg, Virginia, whom he remembered from New York City. The South too produced its prostitutes, many of them probably driven to the occupation by the poverty the war created. One northern soldier reported from Sewanee, Tennessee, that the women "were very fond of Coffee." "They would pay $4.00 per pound for it and for four [grams] of it you could get a good *diddle*." Keokuk, Iowa, where Cyprus Boyd had condemned the visits of soldiers to brothels, was only one of many wide-open cities. For example, in both Nashville and Memphis, the provost marshals licensed prostitution as a health measure. An Ohio private recalled of Nashville's district, Smokey Row, "there was an old saying that no man could be a soldier unless he had gone through Smokey Row . . . The street was about three fourths of a mile long and every house or shanty on both sides was a house of ill fame. Women had no thought of dress or decency. They said Smokey Row killed more soldiers than the war." A Connecticut soldier, reflecting on Alexandria—a town he described as full of brothels—wrote, "We read in the Bible of Citys being distroyed on account of the wickedness in them. if they were destroyed now alexandria wouldent Stand one day longer."[2]

Arguably, prostitutes increased respect for "true women" as contrast was required to define the role of a lady. Just as arguably, prostitutes diminished the overall respect for women. Certainly, they provided soldiers with a model of women for whom they felt no respect was due. A piece of doggerel which one soldier copied into his diary provides a rare insight into one attitude that a northern soldier might have toward fornication and the women with whom it was performed.

When a man mounts a woman
it is for a Short time to Stay
His Head is full of nonsense
his Ass is full of play
He mounts her like a Lion
and Gets off like a Lamb
Buttons up his Breeches
and dont care a Dam[3]

The very fact that the woman was willing to have sex made her not worth considering. And in fact, these Civil War prostitutes and other "loose women," northern and southern, would not and could not be celebrated in the postwar era the way that self-sacrificing nurses would. The postwar world would, however, be willing to celebrate another woman—the high-spirited Confederate belle. At the time, however, the northern soldier felt less admiration for these women than postwar legend would have it. Like the prostitutes, these "she-devils" failed to meet the demands of true womanhood; indeed, their passion and demonstrativeness in an era that valued passionlessness made them like prostitutes in northern eyes.

In the years before the Civil War, many Americans believed that the family was in danger. This frightened them because the family had come to be seen as the most fundamental institution of society and of the body politic. Michael Grossberg explains in his *Governing the Hearth* that by the 1840s Americans "began to speak of a 'crisis of the family.'" This "crisis" inspired new laws designed to reform and strengthen the home. "By 1837 legal commentator David Hoffman spoke of 'a reciprocal action and reaction constantly, though almost invisibly, existent between government and our firesides; and, if insubordination reigns in either, it is very certain, in a short time, to obtain in both.'" This was not a prediction of specifically southern secession and rebellion but instead of a general social and political disorder. It shows how Americans linked the family and national politics. Insubordinate children grew up to be insubordinate citizens.[4]

A guide for young women published in Ohio in 1846 made the political implications of bad mothers and poor motherhood explicit. "Were each American female but faithful to her God, her family, and her country, then would a mighty, sanctified influence go forth, through the wide extent of our beloved land, diffusing moral health and vigor." An age that sentimentalized women and feminized virtue so thoroughly might be expected to have few doubts on this score. But the guide Whiggishly continued, "A spirit of insubordination and rebellion to lawful authority pervades our land—and where are these foes to be checked, if not at the fountain head, in the nursery?" Some mothers had failed their children and their country. "Oh! If every American mother had but labored faithfully in that sanctified enclosure . . . then soul submission to constituted authority, as well as to will of God, have been far more prevalent in our land." Inherent in Republican Motherhood was a critique of mothers. Poor motherhood, it had been predicted, would produce rebellion. In 1860 the rebellion appeared.[5]

The abolitionist critique of the slaveholding South had also been a critique of southern domesticity. Slavery, abolitionists argued, destroyed the black family rather than protecting it. Furthermore, it destroyed the white family as well. Fathers, who routinely indulged their sexual and violent passions, could hardly be fit husbands for virtuous women or good examples for impressionable children. Whereas the northern home reared children to be true men, masters of themselves, the southern home raised little tyrants, training them to be masters without self-mastery. Used to doing as they pleased, was it surprising that such tyrants should also be rebels?[6]

The logic of the abolitionist critique led to an attack on southern women, one ideologically consistent with doctrines of true womanhood but emotionally out of sympathy with the sentimentality of the era. Angelina Grimké, a southerner herself, had argued that "the *women of the South* can overthrow this horrible system of oppression and cruelty, licentiousness and wrong." But they didn't. Indeed, some abolitionists extended their condemnation of women to include northerners; in 1856, Mrs. Eliza Lee Follen said, "The mothers in the Free States could abolish slavery; American mothers are responsible for American slavery." But Ronald G. Walters has shown that few "went so far as to expressly blame women for the evil world they were supposed to be able to regenerate." Usually the condemnation of women implicit in the marriage of abolitionism and the cult of true womanhood remained unvoiced.[7]

This reluctance continued into the Civil War era. Clearly, however, the paradigm of Republican Motherhood indicted southern mothers. They were the mothers of traitors, not of good republicans. Other accusations against Confederate women went beyond the reproach inherent in the logic of Republican Motherhood. Propaganda stories presented the image of Confederate women as savages who toasted military victories with wine drunk from goblets made of human skulls. Reconciling the commonplaces of motherhood and domesticity with rebellion—condemning or acquitting Confederate mothers—became an uncomfortable intellectual problem.

In 1863, the Loyal Publication Society, one of the principal propaganda arms of the Union cause, circulated the remarkable "A Few Words in Behalf of the Loyal Women of the United States by One of Themselves." This pamphlet defends northern women against accusations that they supported the cause of the Union with less fervor than southern women supported the Confederate cause. It is as interesting for the images it creates of Confederate women as for the way it fits northern women into mid-century discussions of self-control.

The pamphlet justifies the behavior of northern women by evoking a concept of self-restraint much admired by northern men. Passion itself was suspect; passionlessness had been held forth as an ideal for northern women. Yet now some northern men pointed to passionlessness as if it were a rebuke: "The gist of all that has been said of our deficiency in the present crisis . . . is that we have not shown *passion* enough . . ." Northern women, the pamphlet argues, were less demonstrative in their patriotism, and for that very reason their loyalty was truer than that of southern women. "The feelings of Northern women are rather deep than violent; their sense of duty is a quiet and constant rather than a headlong or impetuous impulse."

It is southern women rather, argues the author, that suffer in any comparison with their northern counterparts. "There is undoubtedly a radical difference between the women of the two sections. We knew it before there was a thought of war (on our part), and we have become still more thoroughly aware of it since." The difference is the unprecedented savagery of southern women. "Many a Southern woman, during this war, has written to husband, brother, or lover, to bring home with him 'a dead Yankee, pickled,' or 'a hand, or an ear, or a thumb, at least,' if he expected to be well received at his return." A startling image: the southern woman, "decorating her person with ornaments made from human bones," demanding her men not only "murder" but mutilate the husbands and sons of the North, with their future reception into her home and presumably her bed as their reward. By employing their sexuality as a threat and a lure, they have misused their womanhood. The image of the southern women adorned with human bones and demanding human blood is cannibalistic—and almost a stereotype of "Africa" as conceived by white Americans.

What created these southern viragoes? The author answers, slavery and ignorance. "The practice of Slavery, with the unsexing and degrading scenes belonging to it," has de-

stroyed the finer feelings in all white southerners, and ignorance has helped ruin poorer white people. "An ignorance so
gross as to despise instruction, must, when it is the heritage
left by mother to daughter, for successive generations, leave
the soul the unresisting prey of degrading passions."

Yet having summoned these she-devils, the author of "A
Few Words in Behalf of the Loyal Women of the United States
by One of Themselves" could not sustain the accusation
against even southern women. The she-devils are not representative, she says; they are "bad women." We need only discuss them because idiotic northern men are holding up these
passionate women as worthy models for northern emulation.
Most southern women surely are quiet, patriotic, Christian
wives, sisters, and mothers, behaving much the same as northern women would behave if they had been so woefully miseduc-
cated politically. They have not forgotten their womanhood.

Even this praise for most southern women—who were
still women even if southern—raises additional questions.
Why on earth, asks the author, are these women quietly, patri-
otically, and in Christian fashion supporting slavery? "They,
having seen slavery, felt it, known its horrors, suffered under
its attendant evils, and learned, so far as they have learned
Christianity, its incompatibility with God's benign law of love,
have deliberately lent themselves and those dearer than life to
them, to the perpetuation of so awful an evil, for the sake of an
idea, however futile, of worldly prosperity!" The crimes of
slavery that particularly outraged the author and which she
held should have outraged her southern sisters were those
against women and family. "The separation of families, the
lashing of women, brutal tortures of young girls from the
most atrocious motives—all these and long list of crimes
and outrages upon humanity, of which these are but speci-
mens, excite no repugnance, it seems, in the minds of Southern
women!"

The author then compounds even that mystery by proclaiming that most southern women, as wives and mothers, oppose slavery. She says, "When they speak their honest sentiments, they tell their Northern friends that it is a greater curse to them and their children than even we suppose." Yet now anti-slavery women were supporting a pro-slavery war—and being pointed to as models of female patriotism. "We are told of the sacrifices they have made in the cause of War—have they ever made a sacrifice in the cause of Truth?" So the war becomes the responsibility not only of "bad women" in the South but good women as well—those self-sacrificing, quiet, Christian women seemingly so like their northern sisters. "If all the women in the rebellious States who disapprove of slavery, and believe it to be an evil and a sin, had, as one voice, remonstrated against this war for its extension and perpetuity, instead of weakly allowing passion to influence them, without regard to principle or conscience, there would have been no war." Indeed, they were not simply bad Americans—they were what was perhaps worse. Thinking they were dutiful wives, they were instead bad wives. "If every Southern wife had done her whole duty to her husband, using the 'still, small voice' to which God has given such power, in persuading him to listen to reason and duty, rather than to the trumpet-blare of a wicked and heartless ambition, what misery might have been saved!" They had betrayed their consciences, their country, and their families. And—as Lincoln said in another context— the war came.[8]

"A Few Words in Behalf of the Loyal Women of the United States by One of Themselves" is a muddle because the author does not happily follow where the logic of her argument takes her. If women are innately virtuous, they can support neither slavery nor secession. If women are supporting slavery and secession, they have failed in their duties as mothers in such a profound way that it calls into question many mid-century assumptions about woman's role. If womanly duty means only supporting whatever crimes on which one's menfolk embark, then there is no meaningful political content to the separate sphere. The author cannot allow the self-sacrifice of southern women to be equated with that of northern women. But it is only with reluctance she can bring herself to judge harshly women who appear to be acting so womanly.

Northern soldiers showed less hesitation in censuring southern women, but they drew many of the same conclusions that the author of "A Few Words" did. The soldiers sometimes argued that Confederate women were more vicious than Confederate men. Indeed, they thought that the viciousness of these women explained the ferocity of the war. They did not accuse the women of causing the war, but they believed that women encouraged the men to continue the war past the point of rational calculation. Sometimes they spoke as if feminine emotion overwhelmed masculine reason. An officer who was captured at Gettysburg remembered bitterly accompanying the Army of Northern Virginia's retreat. In Hagerstown, Maryland, "numerous secessionists" turned out to watch the army and its prisoners march by. One woman congratulated the Confederate officer leading the prisoners, saying "Colonel, that is the way to bring them in." Even given the Union officer's sense of humiliation, his judgment on the woman initially seems extreme. "Blatantly she thus asserted membership in the nasty group of vixens so numerous in the South—hellcats who goaded half-crazed men to greater ferocity and more treason." In his old age Leander Stillwell declared, "'with malice toward none, and with charity for all,' that in my entire sojourn in the South during the war, the women were found to be more intensely bitter and malignant against the old government of the United States, and the national cause in general, than were the men." His conclusion was that their "attitude is probably another illustration of the truth of Kipling's saying, 'The female of the species is more deadly than the male.'"[9]

Laforest Dunham reported his opinions of southern

women. He wrote from Tennessee that "Thare is some good looking girls down heare, union girls that is." Physical attractiveness became equated with ideology through the link of virtue: virtuous women are pretty, virtuous women are pro-Union. Pro-Confederate women, on the other hand, he rhetorically relegated to an other than human sphere, for he went on to say, "We run in contact with a secesh ladie the other day—I ought not to say ladie about a secesh devel." The crime of the secesh devil was her speech: "She cust ous fore and aft bout we have got use to that." Such speech, obviously, was commonplace; Dunham's perceived South was a land inhabited by (presumably) ugly she-devils but where one could occasionally encounter attractive and patriotic girls. Other northerners agreed with Dunham that it was hard to find the fabled "southern ladies." An army surgeon wrote home to his little sister, complaining how the women of the South failed to live up to their reputations. "Southern ladies do not, I find, possess the great refinement and many accomplishments usually attributed them or if possessing do not display them. They excel in nothing but vile and wholesale abuse of the Yankee Nation." He told his sister, "You, my dear little Dud, would never make a good Secesh. Firstly because you have *too little tongue*—and secondly you are too modest and demure. I could trust you in Secessia for years without fear of your turning rebel." Like the author of "A Few Words," he equated self-restraint with unionism, passion with Confederate loyalty.[10]

In April 1862, James T. Miller was detailed to guard Confederate prisoners being sent from Baltimore to Fort Delaware. As the prisoners, most of them Virginians, came out of the jail, Confederate sympathizers crowded the streets. The men in the crowd mainly stayed quiet, and police arrested the two who did not. "But the women cheered for Jef Davis and said God bless the virginians." The women were presuming on their protected status. Miller's reaction was fierce. "i never thought that i should feel like shooting a woman but if our oficers had given us orders to fire I would have shot some of the women of Baltimore if i could have held my gun steady enough." He wanted to kill women.[11]

The soldiers could point to more than speech to condemn Confederate women. For example, one day a "She secesh Devil" fired on some soldiers on patrol; they arrested her and burned down her house. In Holly Springs, Mississippi, "a rather good looking woman" accompanied by her "four little children" asked Cyrus F. Boyd if he could keep northern soldiers from breaking into her room at the Clayton House and murdering her. Boyd told her that he was not a commissioned officer but that she had nothing to fear in any case. Later he learned that "this *same* woman was arrested for *shooting* one of our men who was on guard at the "Clayton House" (2 days ago)." "She cowardly shot him although he was guarding her property." Rufus Mead, Jr., reported that "the citizens and even women fired on our men as they came through" Winchester, Virginia. "Two of the 28th boys were going along together and saw a woman in a 2nd story window fire a pistol and hit one, then clapped her hands with joy but the other immediately fired at her and hit her in the head when she fell headlong to the pavement." In Warrenton, Virginia, a woman requested that she be sent a squad to protect her property. An aide accompanied the three men out of town. One soldier came back and said that there had been guerrillas waiting for them and the other soldiers and the aide had been captured, and, presumably, killed. The German-speaking soldier who recorded this tale of betrayal in his diary added, "They will hang the woman." Southern women seemed deceitfully to conceal murderousness underneath helplessness; they not only confounded the domestic understanding of women's character, but used it to further their misdeeds. In November 1862, Justus Silliman reported that at Haymarket "a short distance above this place one of the Ohio pickets was found dead, shot it was supposed by one of the women who constituted the population of that town." Silliman does not suggest that there was any hard evidence for any woman's guilt. No matter: "for this outrage all the houses in the vicinity were burned and the delicate creatures turned out in the cold and barren land of secession where they will be very fortunate if they subsist through the winter." While only one soldier involved in these incidents actually killed a woman, all of those who described them spoke approvingly of measures that would or might lead to death.[12]

One conclusion that northern soldiers drew from these incidents and others like them was that Confederate women should not be regarded as exemplars of domesticity and feminized virtue. Instead, they were she-devils. Their passionate encouragement of rebellion spurred Confederate men on to war and took away their reason. These women were hysterical, irrational, treacherous. Their misuse of paramount feminine influence parodied the notion of woman's sphere. If southern men represented an older style of masculinity, now in disrepute, southern women summoned older, darker responses to femininity. A woman who failed to fit the model of true womanhood demanded by the ideology of domesticity was prey to be understood by the more traditional interpretation that women were morally inferior to men.

The other conclusion that northern soldiers drew was that these women were enemies. Indeed, as they supported the rebellion with more irrational zeal than their husbands, brothers, and sons, they might be considered even more dangerous enemies than Confederate men. And thinking of them as enemies transformed them from neutrals to fit objects of war—people to be arrested, executed, burned out. In broader terms, they became the people whose will to make war had to be broken. To that extent, the South became feminized.

That the war against the Confederacy became a war against Confederate civilians is well known. By the latter portion of the war, the Union recognized that the war would continue so long as the Confederate army received popular support. Lincoln and others justified emancipation as a war measure which would weaken southern society. The destruction of crops and property, as practiced by Sheridan in the Valley, was designed both to hinder the supply of the Army of Northern Virginia and to hurt civilian morale. The March to the Sea became the most famous example of the war on southern civilians. It is a commonplace that making war on civilians required a shift in attitudes toward non-combatants. The corollary should be acknowledged: making war on civilians specifically required a shift in attitudes toward women. The northern soldiers' acceptance of the guilt of southern women helped to make the transformation to a more destructive war possible.

James T. Miller, the soldier who had wanted to shoot a woman back in Baltimore, recognized that the war had become a war against women and children. He wrote from Virginia that "the emancipation bill is going to ruin Virginia and i suppose it is the same in the other slave states for in Virginia the nigers have been in the habit of doing all the work and now there is good prospect of the citizens starving and i dont care how quick for although it is hard to think of the women and children suffering but then if the men dont want them to sufer let them throw down thier arms and go home and take care of them." He revealed a great deal in this one sentence, both anger and sympathy toward southern civilians. First, he almost gloated that they would starve; then immediately the inhibitions against making war on women asserted themselves, only to be followed by an attempt to shift any blame onto the rebels. But he acknowledged that the Union war effort, which revolutionized southern society, was inevitably going to hurt women and children. Rufus Mead, Jr., admitted that during the March to the Sea, "I rather felt sorry for some women who cried & begged so piteously for the soldiers to leave them a little and for one would not take any from such poor places." But he did not pity them much. "They feel now the effects of their wickedness," he wrote, "and who can sympathize very much with them." Indeed, he was—rhetorically at least—willing to go further than Miller: "Yet after all I don't know but what extermination is our only means now."[13]

These men could countenance violence against women in a way that they would not have before the war. They accepted that women and children might starve and die, that the war might become one of extermination. But while they found themselves able to condone making women suffer, their participation in the process—and the participation of most northern soldiers—remained a step removed. They would help take the food that the women needed to survive or they would burn down the house that provided shelter for the woman and her family. They could advocate war policies which hurt women. They did not want to be personally involved in the direct application of violence against women. What violence they committed against women was both indirect and sanctioned. Neither James T. Miller nor the overwhelming majority of northern soldiers ever realized his fantasy of shooting a woman.

Nonetheless, some soldiers acted violently against southern women, though the violence was sometimes literal and sometimes symbolic. Robert Strong noticed that "generally, with the ladies, the worse the circumstances they were in, the more bitter they were about 'Lincoln's hirelings, Yankee scum, and bluebellied sons of b—s.'" Once when Union soldiers were passing through Rome, Georgia, women on the balcony of "a young lady's seminary" poured kitchen slops and "the contents of chamber pots" on their heads. Understandably provoked, the soldiers took the young women and spanked them on their "bare flesh." Practically, this was mild retaliation indeed. Symbolically, it was sexual violation. And the reasoning with which the soldiers justified the spanking revealed as much: "The boys, to retaliate, said no one but an abandoned woman would do a thing like that. Abandoned woman had no rights that anyone was bound to respect, so they did not respect girls who emptied chamberpots." The language that Strong records "the boys" using—"no rights that anyone was bound to respect"—could have come out of the Dred Scot decision, where the Supreme Court ruled that a black person had no rights a white person was bound to respect.[14]

The logic here came from General Benjamin Butler's so-called Woman's Order, in which he told the women of New Orleans that if they insulted Union soldiers they would be treated like prostitutes. Butler reacted to the behavior of women who believed their sex gave them a license that would have been denied to men. Besides its threat, Butler's order offended Confederates because it identified patriotic women as prostitutes. Their behavior is what caused them to be regarded as women of the town. Instead of celebrating what Confederates thought high-spirited and admirable loyalty, Butler implied it was unseemly, immoral, and illegal. Confederate Alexander Walker thought that "the malice of Butler against females is more bitter and insatiable than that against males." "A placard in his office in large letters bears this inscription: 'The venom of the she adder is as dangerous as that of the he adder.'"[15]

Major Thomas J. Jordan seems to have used the threat of rape routinely to cow southern women. In Sparta, Tennessee, he ordered local women to prepare food for his six hundred soldiers; "upon failure he said he would turn his men loose upon them and he would not be responsible for anything they might do." Fearing rape, the women obeyed. He used the same tactic in nearby Selina, where he told the women if they refused to cook for his men, "they had better sew up the bottoms of their petticoats." When these incidents came up after Jordan's capture by the Confederate army, Jordan denied he had made such threats. But what Jordan was said to have done in

Sparta and Selina was a small scale version of Benjamin Butler's method of governance in New Orleans.[16]

Major John Chipman Gray, admittedly a Brahmin who
tended to believe all westerners were piggish, denounced a
colonel from Indiana for both his lack of sexual restraint and
the way he treated southern women: "Our Indiana Colonel is
still here developing a new nastiness everyday, going to see his
'clean-footed' women and inviting them to dinner. A woman
came the other day for a pass, he told her she might have one, if
she would go upstairs and kiss the field and staff." Before
giving the pass, the colonel insisted that the woman humble
herself, and the form of the humiliation was explicitly sexual.
Indeed, the humiliation inflicted resembled Butler's, for to
receive the pass she had to act as promiscuous as a prostitute.[17]

How often did soldiers go beyond symbolic rape to actual
rape? In *Against Our Will,* Susan Brownmiller characterized
the Civil War as "a low-rape war." She conjectured that the
reason for this was familial; that the war was fought by brother
against brother: "Injunctions against assaulting one's sister or
one's buddy's sister are part of the code of honor among men;
furthermore, anonymity between rapist and victim is an important factor in rape since an unknown woman is more easily
stripped of her humanity." (Of course, most of the women that
northern soldiers had the opportunity to rape were thoroughly
unknown to them.) Brownmiller was most concerned with
rape as a universal in war, and she treated all soldiers at all time
as interchangeable, so her explanation slights the specific ideology of the northern soldier. Brownmiller also neglected the
way that the American ideology of race has served to bind
white people and exclude others—something to which she is
usually sensitive. What was a low-rape war for white women
may not have been a low-rape war for black women. But
Brownmiller's suggestions were meant to be just that. She was
right to pose the question of the low incidence of rape of enemy
civilians in the Civil War as a historical problem.[18]

The first question should be, how do we know? True, there were very few men convicted for rape, but that hardly proves there were very few rapes. Surely there were rapes that went unreported. Probably there were rapes that when reported were ignored by Union commanders. Nonetheless, it is hard to find much evidence for the rape of white women. Even allowing for the cultural inadmissibility of rape as a subject for discussion, it is reasonable to conclude that one reason so few rapes were reported is that very few rapes occurred.

Nonetheless, a few Union soldiers did rape women while they were in the South. In the spring of 1864, a Massachusetts soldier was convicted of raping a sixty year old woman. On April 25, his whole division was called out to watch the hanging of the rapist. Isaac Hadden described the execution. "Some six thousand of us were drawn up in a hollow square around the gallows." Even though Hadden believed that "hanging is the most disgraceful death a soldier can die," he said that "hanging was too good for him." This particular hanging, however, was inept. "When the trap was sprung, his feet touched the ground and three men had to pull him up so as to strangle him." Whether it was the execution itself, the sloppy way it was performed, or the idea of a fellow soldier raping an old woman that disturbed Hadden, he reported that April 25th had been "a hard day for us." Shortly after the war, Mathew Woodruff, who was stationed in Pascagoula, Mississippi, heard that "a young Lady of the village was brutally outraged by one of the collored Soldiers of the 96th USCT." His response shows that the phrase "brutally outraged" was a mere thoughtless commonplace; actually he regarded the rape as neither brutal nor an outrage: "dont think it was verry serious on her part, nor was it mutch regreted, as she has been heard to say since that *she* 'would not have had it done for a Thousand Dollars!'" Any hint that any sum of money would have been sufficient made the raped woman a whore, and Woodruff apparently shared the old belief that whores cannot be raped. He sanctimoniously concluded that "virtue is of great value in this country or any other, but they can't see it here."[19]

Nonetheless, few northern soldiers raped. One reason was the power of domesticity—even soldiers angered by the treason of southern white women found it difficult to attack individual women directly. Another was the power of the social ideal of self-control. True manhood was characterized by sexual restraint not sexual assertion; even mutually agreeable intercourse would have threatened masculine identity. Letting anger toward women break out in unsanctioned violence against women would have been unmanly. In his study of guerrilla warfare and counter-insurgency in Missouri, Michael Fellman notes that there wartime rage came close to encompassing both rape and murder of white women, but almost never crossed the boundary. In this war-within-a-war, most of the restraints on soldiers were self-imposed—and even here the soldiers spared white women violence which they did inflict on others.[20]

Another reason that so few rapes of white women occurred was racial. In both armies, black women seem to have been the victim of choice. A revealing story comes from St. Mary Parish in Louisiana. There soldiers visited the home of "a venerable lady, the head of that numerous and highly respectable family, the relict of a distinguished gentleman." Beyond looting the house and drinking up the wine cellar, they raped some of the slave women. Some of the house slaves hid in the rooms of the white women, only to be dragged out by drunken soldiers. While all this was going on, their attacks on the white women remained strictly verbal. "To the weeping ladies, whom they abused with ribald tongues, and whose tears they derided, one of them, with menacing gestures cried, 'Dry up; we've seen enough of you Southern women's tears.'" When the widow went to the dining room to beg them to at least leave enough food behind for the family, a soldier forced a glass of wine to her lips, and cried out, "Drink, you damned old rebel, drink to the Union." The rest of the soldiers jeered her from the room.[21]

Or consider the burning of Columbia. As capital, Columbia, South Carolina, represented the state; South Carolina, as the leader in secession, represented the cause of the war. When Sherman's men burned Columbia, they punished the city and the South. But it was the black women in Columbia that night that some soldiers treated the worst of all. In *The Destructive War,* Charles Royster writes of the few murders that soldiers committed during the destruction of the city: "They caught black women, whom they stripped, raped, and killed."[22]

Most of the rapes that northern soldiers committed were of black women. Some soldiers blamed black people for the war. Some seemed, however, to believe that the rape of black women was appropriate punishment for white southerners. The soldiers who raped house slaves in St. Mary Parish were also humiliating the "damned old rebel"; the soldiers who raped and murdered in Columbia were also desolating the center of secession. There is the testimony of Union General William Dwight on the conduct of some soldiers in southwestern Louisiana. He reported to General Nathaniel P. Banks that "Negro women were ravished in the presence of white women and children." The crime against black women was not complete without white witnesses.[23]

Brownmiller argues that rape in warfare is a means of destroying "all remaining illusions of power and property for men of the defeated side." "Men of a conquered nation traditionally view the rape of 'their women' as the ultimate humiliation, a sexual *coup de grâce.*" Indeed, she maintains that "rape of a woman in war may be as much an act against her husband or father, for the rapist, as it is an act against the woman's body." And one reason for this, Brownmiller asserts bluntly, is the reason she says men usually object to rape: it violates the property rights of other men.[24]

Not everyone will agree with Susan Brownmiller that

men categorize rape, a crime against women, as a crime against men. Nor have students of war been comfortable discussing rape as an act of war instead of something incidental to war. But Brownmiller's analysis suggests at least some possibilities for understanding why it was black women, not white ones, who were more often raped by northern soldiers. When soldiers in southwestern Louisiana raped black women "in the presence of white women and children," they were, speaking crudely, violating not only the women but the property rights which slaveholders claimed for themselves. They made mockery of the master class's claims of owning and of protecting black people.

Perhaps there was another logic beyond the one that held black people as property. In his study of abolitionism, Ronald G. Waters discusses "the Erotic South." Key to this belief that the South was a place of no restraint, where sexuality was out of control, was one particular image: that of a white man raping a black woman. Much of abolitionist literature had emphasized the victimization of black women as perhaps the most corrupt horror of slavery; this image of rape could be set up in contrast to the northern domestic ideal. When northern soldiers raped black women, they may have felt they were doing no more than southern masters had done before them. They may also have shared the sick logic that insists rape degrades a woman so that she is no longer worthy of the respect due to still chaste women. Once a woman had been abused, she thus became sexually available for any man who wanted her.[25]

When northern soldiers raped black women, they also, of course, made it clear that they could rape the white women if they chose. They did not choose to do so. They may have raped black women as a way of displacing their impulse to rape white women. While any rape violated northern standards of morality, the rape of white women would have been regarded as a worse crime than the rape of women of other races. Perhaps the rape of black women was in some way a symbolic rape of the white women forced to watch or cowering in fear nearby. But it is also worthwhile to consider again Brownmiller's point that rape is "an act against the husband or father," that rape is intended to demoralize the enemy by abusing his property. For that will allow us to weigh the significance of something we have discussed earlier in this chapter: that for many northern soldiers, the white women of the South were not the wives, mothers, and daughters of the enemy—they were the enemy. Even though rape so often leads to the murder of the victim, the social and psychological trajectory of killing an enemy in war simply is not the same as that of raping the enemy's women. The cultural boundary which northern soldiers may have been most tempted to cross, although they rarely did so, was not the one that protected women from rape. It was the cultural boundary which protected them from bloodshed. Thus the status of southern white women as enemy, paradoxically, may have helped make the Civil War "a low rape war." Soldiers like James T. Miller wanted to kill women, not rape them. Conversely, black women were not enemies—which did not, however, save them from rape.

Because the above discussion of rape may have left the impression that rape was somehow characteristic of the northern soldier, it is important to reiterate that the Civil War was remarkable in how little rape took place. In general, the code of manly self-restraint that so many northern soldiers accepted performed admirably in keeping them from rape. Hatred of southern white women did not lead to wholesale rape of southern white women. How much rape did take place, however, remains something not known and perhaps not knowable.

Rape during the Civil War was performed by other than northern soldiers. Joseph T. Glatthaar observes that "a disproportionate number of black soldiers were executed for rape, along with mutiny, and all of the victims were white women." This disproportion has no necessary relationship to the actual number of black soldiers who committed rapes; it might equally well reveal the bias of those white officers who conducted court-martials. Nonetheless, Glatthaar points to three gang rapes of white women by black soldiers which are well documented. Rape of white women by black soldiers might indeed be explained by Brownmiller's suggestion that rape is an act of war intended to humiliate the enemy—in this case, the white masters. Such rapes might also be considered as examples of revenge rapes, such as Soviet soldiers inflicted on German women in 1945. Returning Confederate veterans and later the Ku Klux Klan—the Freikorps of Confederate defeat—raped black women, sometimes specifically to punish "every black Son-of-a-bitch they could find that had ever fought against them."[26]

Most incidents of violence against southern women were petty, but they nonetheless terrified their victims. And while rape or murder of white women remained rare, the violence sometimes exceeded what might probably be termed petty. For example, outside of St. Martinville, Louisiana, Union soldiers beat up a sixty-year-old woman. There was a logic working itself out in this. While it was hard for northerners to justify all these acts, they were part of the larger, grimmer pattern of making war to break the Confederate will. But besides the ways in which these petty incidents fit in with a new conception of war, they also expressed another logic: that of anger no longer constrained by true manhood, that of anger against women.[27]

Ambrose Bierce—who wrote like O. Henry turned vicious—was a Civil War veteran, and he set some of his grotesque stories in wartime scenes. One of these was "Killed at Resaca." It is the story of Lieutenant Herman Brayle, a man with "a gentleman's manners, a scholar's head, and a lion's heart." Brayle was liked and respected by his fellow officers, although they could not help condemning his "one most objectionable and unsoldierly quality. . . . He was vain of his courage." In battle after battle he irritated his fellow officers by needlessly, if bravely, exposing himself to enemy fire. Finally, at Resaca, Georgia, his determination to court danger led to his death and to something more than his death. The general ordered Brayle to deliver a message, and Brayle deliberately rode in front of the enemy's lines instead of the sensible route. Confederates shot at him; Union soldiers, admiring and fearful, rose and returned this fire; the Confederates naturally shot at them as well; and then both Union and Confederate artillery began firing too. Brayle died—heroically but hardly alone.[28]

The narrator of "Killed at Resaca" received Brayle's "soiled Russia-leather pocketbook" when his belongings were divided among his friends. After the war, he discovered a woman's letter in the pocketbook: "The letter showed evidence of cultivation and breeding, but it was an ordinary love letter if a love letter can be ordinary. There was not much to it, but there was something." The "something" was a second-hand accusation of cowardice against Brayle: "Mr. Winters, whom I shall always hate for it, has been telling that at some battle in Virginia, where he got his hurt, you were seen crouching behind a tree," she had written Brayle in July 1862. "I think he wants to injure you in my regard, which he knows the story would do if I believed it. I could bear to hear of my soldier lover's death, but not of his cowardice." Brayle's foolish, ostentatious bravery was explained. The narrator said, "These were the words which on that sunny afternoon, in a distant region, had slain a hundred men." Then he asked: "Is woman weak?"

In the context of World War I, Sandra Gilbert has discussed what she calls "sexual anger directed specifically against women." This was anger felt toward the homefront narrowed into anger against women. Women, some soldiers of the first world war held, had sent the men out to fight, suffer, and die; women were to blame for men's sufferings. Such anger was felt by at least some northern soldiers. After all, "A Few Words in Behalf of the Loyal Women of the United States by One of Themselves" had made sending northern men into the army a feminine responsibility, recommending that northern women "scorn and reject the coward that eludes the draft"; and Andrew Johnson had advised northern women in much the same terms, telling them, "It was better to be a brave soldier's widow than a coward's wife." Bierce expressed this anger in a literary form. John William De Forest complained of the fact that "everybody at the North was passionately loyal, especially those who would not in any chance be called upon to fight." The violence, often muted, sometimes symbolic, against southern women expressed this sexual anger as well.[29]

Sometimes other men made remarks meant to be funny, that revealed a little of this anger. One soldier wrote a woman back home that "if we live to get home we will have one gay time." Then, he continued, conflating war and sex, "we will take the girls through a course of military tactics that will make them wish that there would be another war so that they could get aclear of us again." Then, still in a humorous vein, he went on to confuse sexual aggression toward women with violence toward rebel men: "Well, I expect you will hate us like poison, for we will be so very fierce after being down here shooting men for three years that everybody will fear us, and may the copperheads fear us for we are going to clean them out as soon as we get home." "Fierce" meant both sexually aggressive and murderous; "fear" was an appropriate response for women and traitors; and the joke seems to be that they will deal similarly with the women they want to caress and the men they want to clean out.[30]

The narrator of Bierce's "Killed at Resaca" visited Miss Marian Mendenhall, the woman whose letter had inspired Herman Brayle's foolhardy ride at Resaca. He handed her back the letter she had written Brayle. A stain on the letter startled her, and the narrator told her, "that is the blood of the truest and bravest heart that ever beat." She threw the letter on the fire, explaining, "I cannot bear the sight of blood." She could more easily cause bloodshed than she could stand the sight of blood. As the narrator stood before her, ready to seize the letter from the fire, she asked him, "How did he die?"

Bierce's narrator answered, "He was bitten by a snake."

7

Faith in Our Fathers:
Authority and Reconciliation

IN February 1864, the officers of the 61st Illinois Infantry Regiment wanted the rank and file of the regiment to reenlist—to "veteranize." The soldiers of the regiment were reluctant. Leander Stillwell remembered, thirty years later: "Nearly all of us had been at the front without a glimpse of our home and friends for over two years. We had undergone a fair share of severe fighting and toilsome marching and the other hardships of a soldier's life, and we believed we were entitled to a little rest when our present term should expire." It seemed likely that too few of the 61st would reenlist for it to keep its regimental status. Then the regiment's colonel, Dan Grass, assembled the regiment for a speech. "He began talking to us like a father would talk to a lot of dissatisfied sons." He told them that he knew they wanted to return home to their families, leaving the war behind, and that he could sympathize with their desire. "But boys," the colonel continued, "this great Nation is your father, and has a greater claim on you than anybody else in the world." What was their choice? "This great father of yours is fighting for his life, and the question now is whether you are going to stay and help the old man out, or whether you're going to sneak home and sit down by the chimney corner in ease and comfort while your comrades by the thousands and hundreds of thousands are marching, struggling, fighting, and dying on battle fields and in prison pens to put down this wicked rebellion and save the old Union." Victory was inevitable; their choice was whether they wished to participate in the triumph. The majority of the regiment changed their minds, reenlisted that evening, and the 61st continued its existence.[1]

Northerners liked to think that authority was paternal. The metaphor made sense of authority in ways that pointed to earliest experience. Parental authority was benign authority. Devotion to parents—and thus to parental figures—was something that could be given without shaming a man's independence. It was, indeed, a primary duty. Much of the power of patriotism came from the identification of loyalty to the government with filial reverence. Beyond legitimizing governmental authority, the parental metaphor made rebellion a primal sin. It identified political disaffiliation with personal betrayal, turning rebels into people who disobeyed the biblical commandment to honor one's father and mother. Ezra Mundy Hunt, the Metuchen, New Jersey, author of "About the War. Plain Words to Plain People by a Plain Man," clearly wanted to put the case for the Union and the administration into homely language. He chose the language of the family. He summarized the sectional conflict and the subsequent rebellion as a family tragedy. "If a feud should occur in a family," Hunt said, "and two out of six children should rebel against parental authority, while the other four are disposed to think their father and mother about as good caretakers as they could expect under any change, it would clearly be the part of wisdom in the dutiful children to adhere to the old folks, rather than break up the family and see what would come out of the ruin." After the firing on Fort Sumter, the *Pittsburgh Post,* a Democratic newspaper, demanded that the government's "power to punish, as well as to protect its children, be used."[2]

Americans imagined governmental authority as parental; how did they understand parental authority? Mary Ryan describes antebellum child-rearing manuals. "A good parent mingled his own regret and pain with each act of punishment," she explains, adding, "Once the child had begged for forgiveness, and adequately demonstrated his repentance, the affectionate bonds could be swiftly restored." She quotes from one manual, which advised this treatment of a disobedient child: "Let him throw himself in your arms, kiss him, and tell him you hope he will never be naughty again, for if he is you must punish him, and it makes you sorry to punish him." This sentimental manipulation was part of the prewar shift of child-rearing from father to mother. As Ryan says elsewhere, "Put simply, love had vanquished force and authority, the female had replaced the male, in the social relations of childrearing."[3]

Northerners often spoke in terms of mild paternal authority, associating it particularly with Lincoln. In 1864, a committee of the United States Sanitary Commission issued a report on conditions in rebel prisons. The committee contrasted the harsh treatment the rebels inflicted on their prisoners with the gentle treatment that the Union government offered its prisoners. The reason for the difference, they argued, came from the nature of the rebellion. Rebels, motivated by race and class prejudice, acted like brutes. The motivation of the Union government, however, was far more Christian. The committee asserted of the Union government that "no sentiment of anger or resentment has actuated it from the beginning." In other words, the Union government acted paternally, dealing out necessary discipline without hatred. Perhaps this view—even though it hardly reflected the realities of the bitter struggle—also influenced the genuinely and almost inexplicably benign treatment of the rebels after the war was over.[4]

During the war, however, a great many northerners were

not sorry to punish rebels. The demands of so severe a war made the mildness of parental authority unattractive. As early as spring 1862, Felix Brannigan, a soldier in McClellan's army, rejected the paternal model's suitability for the South. He was confidant of Union victory, but not of sectional reconciliation. "We can conquer their resistance (vie & armis) but what can overcome their hatred? The merciful forbearance of the Government—such as a father extendes to a loved child—should work a cure; but alas! in too many instances under my own observation it has signally failed." So much for McClellan's soft war. "Rebellion and ingratitude, twin sisters in this unnatural struggle leads them on to destruction!" Forbearance being inappropriate, Brannigan called for harsher measures to win the war: "tho' we had to *exterminate* our Brethren of the South in accomplishing it!" Not very paternal, nor very brotherly. But even as Brannigan rejected paternal forbearance, he could not escape familial imagery when he discussed the South. The government had been offering fatherly forgiveness, rebellion and ingratitude were twin sisters, southerners were brothers to northerners, and warfare between the sections was "unnatural"—against nature.[5]

Northerners also judged this rebellion against parental government and the natural order to be ultimately a rebellion against an even more powerful and just father: God. Volunteer General Robert McAllister wrote home of the "long lines of artillery and cavalry and infantry" that "move along over hill and dale, carrying with them the destructive weapons to put down this wicked rebellion and teach the Southerners with force what they would not learn in time of peace—that governments are not so easily broken up, and that God requires obedience to law and order." The implements of destruction were the implements of instruction; force was God's means of persuasion. McAllister used this lesson to amend thoroughly the traditional meaning of the United States' role in history. Where Americans had hoped that their country's example was one of liberty, McAllister held the nation up as an emblem of power. "And though we are passing through a sore trial, and our nation is suffering a terable calamity, our government will yet stand before the world in all its former grateness as a tower of strength—teaching rebellious spirits in all nations that governments and their power come from God." McAllister's United States was no longer a pattern for revolution but the model of godly obedience.[6]

Not all soldiers agreed with the logic of godly obedience. Albinus Fell, for example, complained when a colonel with a ministerial background—"a dam old servant of god that lied for him for several years"—employed this logic in a sermon to Fell's regiment. "he proved that we wer all Secesh and that we had seceded from Gods Government and that the devil was our leader." This sort of pious browbeating offended Fell—"he dont like our boys but God knows there is no love lost (if he dont I will tell him the first time I see him)."[7]

More pious soldiers emphasized that the war was divine punishment for national sins. After experiencing the bloody battles of the Seven Days, Union soldier John S. Copley called for national submission to God. More than ever, he wanted an end to the war and a chance to return to his home—"Home, ever dearer to me, has its blessings immeasurably enhanced." For peace to come, there must be "an acknowledgment of Gods dealings with us because of our great national and individual sins. . . . But one thing is required my dear friend to that consummation—that is until we as a nation and as individuals acknowledge this and repent of our sins and turn to God and respect his laws I cannot expect this strife to cease." God and God alone had saved the Army of the Potomac in the late battles, Copley announced—so much for McClellan's claims of masterful retreats and changes of base—and only God could bring peace. The war itself was God's dealing with the American people, a means of disciplining those who had fallen away and forcing them to recognize divine authority. Copley prayed that the United States would become a literally "Godfearing nation." Burage Rice predicted that, while the rebellion's failure was inevitable, the war would continue as long as necessary "to punish us as a wicked nation for our sins."[8]

Some thought the war meant God brooked no challenge to His authority; others that He brooked no challenge to any constituted authority. When Justus M. Silliman and his fellow soldiers in the Seventeenth Connecticut heard of Lincoln's murder, they concluded that its ultimate cause was divine will. God took Lincoln from the world so that men would look not to other men but to God. Indeed, according to Silliman, the death of Lincoln was a product of a quarrel over precedence between a superior patriarch and his inferior. "Then we reflected that our cause was still in the hands of the Supreme Ruler who has thus far guided us through our troubles, and that he might have removed from us the Father of our Country that we might be induced to place our whole reliance on the God of our fathers, and not in man as perhaps has been done by a large portion of our people." Father Abraham was gone, but fatherly authority still reigned.[9]

Judging from Leander Stillwell's memories of his regiment's reenlistment, northern soldiers found the metaphor that associated governmental authority with parental authority persuasive: it could motivate their service. As discussed earlier, many volunteers had understood the war as familial; it was an effort to defend both their own homes and the legacy of the Revolutionary generation, the so-called Fathers. Yet the process of fighting this war, paradoxically, created contradictions within the notion of fatherly authority. Just as the war envisioned as a defense of family and community took soldiers away from their families and communities, the war to vindicate the parental authority of the union sometimes led men to question the judgment of their own fathers.

Insofar as there was a northern intellectual rebellion in response to the Confederate political rebellion, it was, oddly enough for a rebellion, one in favor of more authority. Sons challenged their fathers' political wisdom to demand more governmental authority. That the Civil War represented a move toward authority has been demonstrated already. Indeed, this is the principal line of argument in George Fredrickson's respected *The Inner Civil War*. Lori D. Ginzbergs's study of women's benevolent societies also suggests a shift in attitudes toward authority during the era of the Civil War. "The themes that pervaded efforts at sustaining the soldiers (and, to a less extent, the freed slaves) contrasted sharply with those of an earlier age: nationalism, discipline, centralization, and, above all, efficiency became the watchwords of a new benevolence." These values were also embraced by the soldiers.[10]

Northern soldiers called for a stronger national government because they wanted a more vigorous prosecution of the war. Like most American volunteers, they wished for a quick war and a decisive victory. They demanded a government willing and able to achieve such a victory. They were also willing, grudgingly, to pay the butcher's bill. They recognized bitterly that this unprecedented destructive war meant they would die in greater numbers than anyone had imagined in 1861. In November 1864, Hermon Clarke, a prewar Democrat who was no friend of the administration or of General U. S. Grant, pointed out what the commonplace phrase "vigorous prosecution of the war" really meant. "It means every week or two take out a few thousand men and butt them against the mud walls that surround Richmond, then march back to camp with from five to fifteen hundred [fewer] men than we went out with!" Yet Clarke himself is an example of how soldiers came to laud national authority and to reject the political counsels of the generation before them.[11]

Hermon Clarke served in a New York regiment. His war

experience forced him to change his attitudes toward national policy in ways that his Democratic father back home had trouble understanding. This change led him simultaneously to support the authority of the national government and to challenge his father's patriarchal authority. December 1863 found him writing his father that "I think some of your ideas in regard to the conduct of the war are very good, but I reckon you are a little mistaken in some respects." His father had charged that the army only let soldiers who would vote Republican go home for elections. Clarke denied this and explained that the reason "there were not more Democrats home" from the army was "they are a very scarce article in the Army at present. . . . The past six months have made a great change politically in the Army. Men who a year ago were bitterly against the Administration have failed to find even sympathy, much [less] encouragement in any other party." Clarke anticipated his father's objection; his father would certainly reply that the soldiers had not received support from the Administration either. "I think they have. At least they haven't received open opposition from it, and they have from all other parties." Clarke then rehearsed a soldier's list of grievances against the Democrats: the Vallandigham affair, the New York draft riots, the opposition to recruiting black men into the army, the encouragement to draft dodging. Had Clarke stayed at home with his father, none of these would have offended him as much; he had been a good Democrat. As a soldier, however, he regarded them as measures against his own interests. "I do think the Democratic party has gone back on the soldier." As a soldier, he repudiated his father's politics. His conclusion was that the war required the very measures that the Democratic party was denouncing as revolutionary. "Truly the people of the North ought to take hold of this Rebellion and put it down—but no! they won't do it. They are afraid of something—I don't know what. It may be bullets. But instead of coming out when called, they must stand and quibble on some

point of law while the enemy is gaining on us. Now, law and
the Constitution can't put this rebellion down; it has got to be
done by fighting."[12]

Clarke believed that his status as a soldier gave him the
moral authority to question his father's judgment. The war
shifted moral authority from fathers to sons; the question
"what do we owe the soldiers?" joined "what do we owe our
parents?" as moral touchstones. When Tennessee Unionist
Andrew Johnson addressed a mammoth political rally in Indiana, a state with strong Copperhead proclivities, he asked,
"Will you deny that your soldiers' blood has been shed in a
glorious cause? If you do, you are unworthy fathers and
mothers." To be sure, many soldiers were already self-reliant
adults, and those of the "boys" who really were barely out of
boyhood would have soon left the homes of their fathers in any
case. The experience of breaking away from parental discipline
was inevitable, but for many young men between 1861 and
1865 it occurred in the context of military service, bitter politics, and an increasingly destructive war.[13]

Other, figurative, fathers were also challenged. If any of
the Revolutionary generation lost credibility in the North because of the war, it was Thomas Jefferson. In 1861, future
President James Garfield ruled that secession proved that
Jefferson was wrong and Alexander Hamilton right. He made
a speech arguing that "Jeffersonianism was now fully tested
and had proved a failure," and that "Hamilton was right in his
main propositions." Now, the Jefferson he referred to was in
particular the Jefferson of the Kentucky Resolutions, which
Garfield thought had introduced the dangerous ideas of nullification and secession into American political discourse. But
Garfield went beyond rejecting secession when he embraced
the Hamiltonian vision for the United States. Jefferson—as
slaveholder, the southern author of nullification, and an advocate of democracy that had struck federalists of his era as Jac-
obinical and licentious—had little allure for many northerners

of the Civil War era. When John Lothrop Motley defended the
Union in the London *Times,* he identified "the most venerated
expounders of the Constitution" as "Jay, Marshall, Hamilton,
Kent, Story, Webster"—Federalists and Whigs all. Never
properly one of the Founding Fathers in any case, Jefferson
lost a great deal of his authority during the war. The Congre-
gational minister Horace Bushnell attacked Jefferson's Decla-
ration of Independence for putting American nationality on
the false basis of the social contract, consent of the governed,
and natural rights. In *The Inner Civil War,* George Fredrickson observes that in the judgment of some wartime
thinkers "Thomas Jefferson, with his defense of Shays' Rebellion and his advocacy of a revolution every twenty years, was
rejected as a philosopher of 'Americanism.'" [14]

The ways in which good Unionists conceived the war
could seem diametrically opposed. There were those who saw
the war as a war against tyrants and for liberty. There were
those who saw it as a war against rebels and for authority. In
fact, most Unionists would have agreed with both of these
propositions—the key being that legitimate authority rested
with the people. But some men stressed the need to establish a
nationwide respect for authority more than others. This split
was hardly coterminous with any split between officers and
ranks. Aristocratic pretensions and conservative sentiments
were not prerequisites for wanting the government strengthened. In January 1863, Burage Rice, who had served as captain of a New York regiment, said, "We never can prosper till
stubborn leaders learn to listen to and yield to the will of
People. The people are not fools though they do not live in
palaces or were not 'born to govern.'" David Nichol advocated
mutual respect as the proper relationship between officers and
men; he also came to advocate a tough war policy with a strong
military administration. "We must take the thing as it is," he
wrote his father, "read the traitors out at home first before
going south; suppress the papers & keep the politicians out of

this war; put fighting Generals at our head & then we will put down the rebellion & not till then." Beyond that he supported Lincoln's recent Emancipation Proclamation: "I am no nigger worshipper but it has become a military necessity." Yet with all this call for a vigorous war effort, Nichol had not lost his distrust of officers. "Is the officer actuated by the Love of Country?" Nichol asked. "Is he true to the Flag he took a solemn oath to protect[?]" His answer? "far from it.—he is fighting for pecuniary motives to get his hands a little deeper in Uncle Sam's pockets, wants promotion and his name printed in every paper throughout the country."[15]

Paul Oliver was much more socially prominent than Hermon Clarke or David Nichol; indeed he was a correspondent of Dudley Fields. But like Clarke, Oliver was out of sympathy with the radicals, whom he believed betrayed his beloved General McClellan. Yet instead of arguing for the traditional Democratic governmental restraints, Oliver's distrust of the radicals led him to call for national authority to be strengthened. He pronounced the Confederacy "an *absolute military despotism.*" It could put all its white men in arms—Oliver believed in the reality of those phantom numbers that continually intimidated McClellan—while in 1862 the North still depended on enlistments. His conclusion? "If the North wants to put an end to this war, it had better put its shoulder to the wheel, & draft at once, yes without a moment's delay." Without this, the Union armies would always be outnumbered. "For I tell you the enemy is not idle & all this year may bring another 300000 men in the field, he can best you in numbers in the same space of time, unless you adopt the same system, & draft men." Yet this "same system" was the one he had labeled a "military despotism." "The military despotism now prevailing in the South is the most complete for military success possible."[16]

When some men spoke of the war as a disciplinary measure, they included the whole nation in their prescription. For example, Isaac Jackson had more than southerners in mind

when he asserted the principle of obedience to those in authority. Referring to pro-Vallandigham demonstrations back in
Ohio he said, "I am very sorry to learn that any disturbance
should occur between the citizens and soldiers, but the people
must learn to obey the laws." He continued: "They must be
obeyed. If no other way, force must be used." Consequently,
he could imagine cheerfully the application of military force
against his own people as well as those of the South. "And it
would give me as much pleasure to put down Rebellion at
home as down here in the South."[17]

Respect for law and national authority was one result of
the Civil War, as was the willingness to sanction a more coer-
cive state. It is not surprising that the war to vindicate the
authority of the government should rapidly become a war to
increase the authority of the government. What is noteworthy
is that in this war, it was often the sons who called for stronger
government, more respect for the laws, and the squashing of
dissent. As soldiers, they claimed for themselves the moral
authority to determine what the true needs of the nation were.
Their sacrifices, they argued, gave them the right to speak for
the nation; their wartime experience gave them the perspi-
cacity to see that the nation and its government must be
strengthened. In advocating a more powerful government,
they often challenged the political wisdom of their fathers.

What was to be done with the South once the war was
over? Clearly, the answer would be principally a matter of law,
politics, power, and ideology, a balancing of northern anti-
rebel sentiment with northern racism, a long process in which
southerners both black and white would affect the decision.
But the centrality of the family metaphor to northern culture
meant that it too emerged in odd places to influence the course
of reconstruction, to give northerners some symbols of what

was just and what was possible, and to explain the final conclusion.

The generational metaphor that expressed the sectional conflict—that of parents and children, some dutiful and some wicked—was probably the most common familial metaphor that explicated the body politic. But one other was available, less as a way of describing conflict and more as a means to presage ultimate sectional reconciliation. In some respects, this metaphor drew on the most obvious meaning of Union: it equated the reconciliation of North and South with the union of marriage. In this metaphor, the North appeared as the husband and the South became that husband's future wife.

Among its other strengths and weaknesses, John William De Forest's *Miss Ravenel's Conversion from Secession to Loyalty* can be read as a veritable handbook to notions of masculinity, true manhood, and woman's nature. The situation which lies at the center of the book is the competition between two styles of manliness—the old aggressive masculinity and the new restrained true manhood—as they are embodied in two men who love the same woman. Yet this situation also serves in some ways as a metaphor for the conflict which underlies the war itself. The "prize," whom both men win successively, is Lillie Ravenel, a New Orleanian. Miss Ravenel, as the title indicates, is a secessionist. "Now Miss Ravenel was a rebel. Like all young people and almost all women she was strictly local, narrowly geographical in her feelings and opinions." This novel of courtship and war is also a novel of her most unpolitical political conversion.[18]

The two rivals are Lieutenant Colonel Carter of Virginia and Edward Colburne of New Boston—i.e., New Haven. A Unionist, Carter is also a southerner and an Old Army man—and a "full-blown specimen of the male sex." He drinks and fornicates to excess—which is, in Colburne's and De Forest's terms, to say he drinks and fornicates. He cannot restrain his impulses; in fact, his two worst vices are ones in which by definition a man loses self-control. Yet he is the man who initially attracts Miss Ravenel, marries her, and then betrays her. He cannot resist the dark Creole sexuality and subtlety of the wicked and charming Mrs. Larue. Consequently, his masculinity can lead him only to a broken home and heroic death on the battlefield.[19]

Colburne represents northern manliness—a little uncertain of itself as the war begins, but ultimately the stuff Union victory is made of. The war develops Colburne. It makes him and the North at large more manly. Making allowances for his penchant for the occasional "segar," Colburne is a model of restraint; as his name suggests, he indeed bears himself coolly—or perhaps was born coolly. Miss Ravenel regarded him as "very pleasant, lively and good; but—and here she ceased to reason—she felt that he was not magnetic." Until Miss Ravenel has become Mrs. Carter—until she has been chastened by childbearing, warfare, betrayal, and grief—she cannot appreciate the cooler northern virtues of Edward Colburne.[20]

Herein lies the problem. Miss Ravenel's conversion is motivated not by her intellect but by her loyalties and other passions. Her secession is presented as purely a product of her Louisiana upbringing—despite the fact her father is a southern Unionist. Her conversion to loyalty is the result of her loyalty first to her father and then to her husband Colonel Carter. It is not of the mind but of the heart. And De Forest does not portray Lillie Ravenel's loving nature and lack of intellectual comprehension as unique. They are instead the result of the very thing that makes her desirable—her womanhood.

"Woman is more intimately and irresponsibly a child of Nature than man."[21] As children of nature, women can have loyalties, but not ideologies. For example, Miss Ravenel's support of the institution of slavery is partially explained by the fact she was not "nurtured in the truly free and democratic North." But De Forest also explains it by reference to an innate female nature: "all women love aristocracies."[22] When Carter receives a promotion, he dampens Lillie's enthusiasm by explaining "'I am only a general while the war lasts.' . . . 'But the war will last a long time,' hopefully replied this monster in woman's guise, who loved her husband a hundred times as much as she did her country." And when Carter goes on to say the promotion means his return to the field, Lillie begs him to stay with her instead. Carter chides her, "My darling, you want to make a woman of me. . . . I must show myself a man, now that my manhood has been recognized. My honor demands it." De Forest has long demolished any notion of Carter's honor—he is a drinker, a womanizer, and now a swindler. He also demolishes any political content to Miss Ravenel's conversion from secession to loyalty. She cannot form ideologically based allegiances—she can only love men.[23]

Unlike the southern women portrayed in "A Few Words in Behalf of the Loyal Women of the United States by One of Themselves," Miss Ravenel is a modest, tractable wife. Insofar as Colonel Carter can be led toward good, she leads him—only to have Mrs. Larue lead him away. She cannot stay with him after she learns of his infidelity, but she refuses to condemn him. Marrying a Unionist makes her a Unionist; she does not subvert his unionism. But she is without question a southern woman. It is her southernness, not just her femininity and his masculinity, that makes her respond to Carter. Indeed, as a southerner, she was familiar with Carter's style of masculinity and found it attractive rather than repulsive. When Colburne joins the army, Miss Ravenel is initially annoyed but quickly reconciles herself: "after the fashion of most Southern women, she believed in fighting, and respected a man the more for drawing the sword, no matter for which party." Her father frequently teases her about "Ashantee English," by which he means her use of black idioms, thus linking Miss Ravenel's southernness to Africanness. In a novel linking politics, war, and gender roles, Miss Ravenel is the feminized South.[24]

Portraying the South as a woman to be courted and won to loyalty became a common figure in postwar fiction; what is startling about De Forest's use of this device is how early it appears: *Miss Ravenel's Conversion* was finished by autumn of 1865. Romances between southern belles and Yankee officers would appear in popular fiction throughout the period of sectional reconciliation; indeed, they represented sectional reconciliation. Instead of she-devils, southern women became objects of romantic conquest. In these postwar romances, the northern perception of the South as irrational and passionate—and thus feminine—became softened; indeed, these stories and novels translated southern emotionalism into a capacity for love and loyalty. This form of fiction did not so much depoliticize women—women were already viewed in some ways as apolitical—as it used inherently apolitical women to depoliticize the South. Thus, novels like *Miss Ravenel's Conversion* made reconciliation imaginable by making wifely devotion a metaphor for the South's reintegration into the nation.[25]

Even during the war itself, when many northern soldiers believed that southern women were the worst rebels, there was something of a tendency to conflate intimacy between northern men and southern women with conquest and reconciliation. Attraction, sexual and otherwise, between men and women could be based on many things other than shared convictions about the nature of the Union and secession. Northern soldiers and southern white women did socialize, even court. In Selma, Alabama, in April 1865, E. N. Gilpin noted that "the fair ladies of Selma are busying themselves feeding and caring for the captured Rebs. . . . The boys sympathize with the 'Jonnies' and as a consequence walk home with the girls." S. H. Eels reported from Middleburg, Tennessee in 1863 that "There have been a good many marriages down here in Dixie between the soldiers and Southern girls. more than one would expect from the difference in sentiment." Eels described these marriages in language with mild overtones of possession as one of the conqueror's rights: "An old nigger expressed it well when he said the 'Yankees done took all the corn and horses and niggers in the country, killed off all the men, and now I believe 'fore God they goin' to marry all de widders.'" (Eels had earlier joked, "Wouldn't a wife be a good memento of the campaign?") Yet his conclusion was framed more in terms of the domestic ideology. "If this war should ever end, a great many of our soldiers will certainly stay down here and their being here will undoubtedly help a great deal to keep the country loyal." The resettlement of the South with loyal men—and the submission of southern women to loyal husbands—would make the South itself loyal, placing Union voters at the ballot boxes and Union families at southern hearths. And if southern women did love loyal men, many of the strengths they displayed in supporting Confederate husbands could once again be regarded as admirable. Immediately after the war, Corporal Rudolphe Rey wrote Miss Lizze De-Voe that he admired the "spunk" of Jefferson Davis's wife. Varina Davis did show "spunk," doing her best to care for her husband while he was in captivity. Rey told Devoe that "that is the kind of woman i want to get a hold of (ahem)." After all, if a woman's duty was to love her husband, both Varina Davis and Lillie Ravenel Carter Colburne had succeeded.[26]

Other northern soldiers conducted more cynical courtships. While stationed in Maryland, Frank Roberts wrote a friend: "The boys like it very well here and pitch into the gals heavy." Perhaps that was why health in the company was good—except for a half-dozen cases of clap. Roberts himself, however, had balked at getting involved with the local women: "As for myself, I have not seen a girl that I like well enough to go with and another and a stronger reason is that the a—s of my britches are entirely wore out." He also reported that "Seth

Smith is married to a woman old enough to be his mother and ugly as blue mud." Smith's marriage conceivably was like the ones that a Confederate soldier warned about: Southern women "marrying" Yankees only to be thrust aside when real wives show up.[27]

Treating rebels as fit subjects for marriage hollowed out much of Republican Motherhood—as the Loyal Women of the North had recognized when they employed notions of domesticity to criticize southern women. Obedience to husbands by itself was not sufficient basis for mothers to perform their duties toward their children and their country. Nor were formerly Confederate wives likely candidates for Republican Motherhood. Furthermore, squeezing issues of sectional reconciliation into a model of courtship and marriage was hardly satisfactory as a representation of how specific issues should be compromised. Nonetheless, casting the sections as husband and wife did suggest that the North and South were a family and that their differences would have to be resolved within the familial context. What is most surprising about using courtship and marriage as the image of sectional reconciliation is that sometimes soldiers like S. H. Eels could articulate this understanding in the midst of war itself.

Generally, however, the metaphor of courtship and marriage standing for the relationship between the sections was more customary in the postwar era. The more common familial image during the war was that which characterized the national government as parental, the rebellious states as bad children, and the loyal as dutiful ones. This identification added an emotional force to the concept of the Union. Like the metaphor of sectional marriage, it also influenced the way in which some northerners perceived the problem of reconstructing the union. If the southern states were disobedient children, should they be treated in ways congruent to parents disciplining their children? The parental image of the national government not only legitimized crushing the rebellion but forgiving the rebellious as well. This too was part of the family metaphor for politics—the notion of the Union as a forgiving parent.[28]

With the family metaphor at the center of northern understanding of the American political system, ultimate sectional reconciliation looks close to inevitable. As early as April 1861, the *Boston Post,* calling for war against the South, looked forward to a postwar era when the United States might "see PEACE in her borders, and all her children loving each other better than ever." If the Union was thought of as a family, the erring brethren must be restored for the family to be complete. The southern states too would return to the table—although not the head of the table—to reclaim their vacant chairs. Unfortunately, black people were not commonly included in the image of the nation as one large family. When North and South were reconciled, it was done at the expense of roughly half the people who lived in the South. The postwar family reunion welcomed white southerners as poor relations and recognized black southerners as, at best, only distant kin.[29]

8

"Going Home"

PRIVATE Laforest Dunham spent much of the war homesick. By his own confession, he had been a careless boy who
worried little about home and familial duties. The war and the
deaths of those close to him had changed that. "Tell the truth I
never new what home was till now." Consequently, he promised his family and himself that he would return home if he
survived and never leave again. "If I ever get out of this show
alive and well, I never will get so far from home but what I can
heare the first rattle for dinner." At times, thoughts of home
reduced him to tears.

The military experience reconciled Dunham to a place
and life he previously had disdained. "I use to complain about
Illinois but I think I can be satisfied if I ever get back again."
His new ambition was to settle down on an eighty-acre farm
back home. "I tell you what if I ever get back I calculate to go
to farming and stay there. I have got enough of romeing this
kind any how." While Dunham never quite says so in his
letters home, I suspect that his dissatisfaction with Illinois and
longing to "rome" had helped motivate his enlistment. "I use
to talk about being away from home when I was thare," he
wrote, "but little did I know what it was till now." Now, to

135

imagine a future, he could only imagine his past. "Would that I could be in old Ill. guiding a plow."

He also imagined himself a dutiful son. "Would that evry boy knew what I know now. They would never speak a cros word to thare parents." He lectured his brother Hiram on the need to stay out of the army and to support their parents. "Hiram be kind to your father and mother and help them all you can and you never will be sorry for it." He urged Hiram to learn from his mistakes. "I have often thought about when I use to do rong and Pa or Ma would talk to me and tell me I would be sory for it some day, but I could not see it then or pretended so but I can see it now." He said that if Hiram had been through his experiences, he would say, "O if I was at home in my Pas house and in a good bed that my dear mother made how nice it would be." He promised his sister Hercey, "iff I ever get back you will never want for a kind and loving brother."

Thoughts of home obviously made Dunham miserable, but they also obviously sustained him through the war. By concentrating his thoughts on home, family, "normal life", and his prewar existence, he insulated himself somewhat from his wartime experience. As poet David Jones did with his World War I experience, Dunham succeeded in placing his wartime life "in parenthesis." Perhaps he had enlisted seeking "real life"; now he concluded that real life was what he had lived in before and would live in again after the war. This recourse, this dreaming of home, characterized not just the experience of the northern soldier but the experience of many soldiers at many times in many wars. By looking at Laforest Dunham it is possible to see that this longing is not simply a natural affection but a reaction to war; to go further, it is in some ways a psychological construct necessary to cope with the war experience. And if it was a psychological construct, it was one made from handy cultural materials as well as from personal history.

Laforest Dunham was lucky. He survived the war and

was able to return home. Dunham rejoined his family, the focus of his wartime emotion. Then he left them behind and moved to Iowa, where he lived the rest of his life. Once he was back from the war, his peacetime frustrations with Illinois could resurface—although he stayed a farmer. His all-consuming desire for home had been a stratagem of war. The war over, he was free to leave it behind. The reality that had created the strong attachment to home turned out to be the war, not home itself. The nostalgia had served its purpose: psychological survival.[1]

Laforest Dunham had gone to war with an older brother, Albertus. Albertus did not survive the war. In January 1863, he died of "brain fever"—encephalitis. "He was out of his head most of the time during his sickness," his brother reported. In his delirium, he imagined he was at home or that his wife came to visit him. "When he was in his write mind he wanted me to read the Bible to him." His brother and his other fellow soldiers buried him in a Methodist cemetery near Fountain Head, Tennessee—"a romantic looking place" and "whare the first confrence Meating was heald west of the Mountains." As well as he could, Laforest buried Albertus according to nineteenth-century desires that cemeteries be lovely, picturesque places, from which one could draw aesthetic pleasure and moral lessons. The cemetery at Fountain Head had both natural beauty and historic associations. "The boys in the company got a nice hed board and set out to nice cedar treas, one at the head and one at the foot, and Delos Robinson and myself made a fence around it." In the parlance of the day, Albertus Dunham had gone home to heaven.[2]

One of the clichés of historical and cultural analysis is that World War I, with its unprecedented bloodletting, produced widespread disillusionment. This may or may not be true. But it should provoke a question—Why was there no similar mass disillusionment in the United States in the years after 1865? Roughly 360,000 Union soldiers died during the war— approximately 17 percent of the 2,1000,000 men who served in the army.[3] How did Americans cope with the deaths caused by the Civil War? No easy question to answer, and not one that any one answer will satisfy. For the North, part of the answer can be found in the way that meaning was successfully attributed to death. Another part of the answer is the way that death itself was domesticated. Both developments relied heavily on northern imagery of the home and the family.

The first and most obvious influence on attitudes toward death was Christianity. Many soldiers—most literate soldiers, judging from their written remains—were believers. Death and its fears had already been assuaged by faith before the war brought mass killings. Other soldiers converted to Christianity under the stress of war. "In God is my trust," Benjamen F. Ashenfelter assured his mother, "I fear not to Die." "God is indeed the only refuge of the soldier," wrote Frederick Pettit. When he first came to the army, Pettit feared the impact of war on soldiers. "It makes men wicked." Indeed, he held his fellow soldiers in low enough regard that he could write, "I dread to see the day when this army goes home. Religion will be driven from the country." But he soon decided he found it "as easy to serve God here as at home." Despite the coarse and wicked soldiers he met, he saw a hope of moral reformation that attended military service. "Disappointment, danger, and temptation seem to drive me nearer the cross." Service would make him "a better Christian."[4]

There were, as Pettit learned, unbelievers among the soldiers. Rufus Mead, Jr., wrote, "I sometimes shudder at the thought that so few of our Regt ever realize that they are immortal beings and hope that now as they are about to face death on the battlefield they may be led to prepare themselves for 'their great and last change.'" Some of those whom Mead worried over probably counted on luck to save them—or, more precisely, could not imagine dying. Albinus Fell delineated this kind of thinking in a letter he wrote his wife. "A great many think they will be the fortunate ones," Fell said. "They think men may be killed by their side but each ones thinks for himself I will escape the leaden hail and be looked up on as a man that feard not to die in our country's cause." Other soldiers were hostile toward religion. "This evening there was a *mock prayer meeting* in Co 'K,'" Cyrus F. Boyd recorded. "They sang and prayed in blasphemous mockery." But northerners made intense efforts to bring these soldiers into the fold. For example, Reuben Smith Goodman served with the U.S. Christian Commission, visiting hospitals in Louisville, Nashville, and Chattanooga, where he labored both to comfort men and to see that they died well. His first day in this occupation, another soldier sent him to "a young man, a boy indeed, named Francis M. Stevenson." Stevenson looked a likely candidate for a good death—he had only a few days to live and he came from a religious family. The minister spoke with him. "He wept while being conversed with, and said he would try to give his heart to the Saviour." Goodman also had hopes of the older man who sent him to Stevenson. Talking to him, Goodman "found he was full of thought, and almost if not quite persuaded to be a Christian." Goodman had to leave the older man, but when he next saw him, he was studying the Bible.[5]

Christianity, even if narrowed to Protestantism, had many different aspects in the mid-nineteenth-century United States. Nineteenth-century American Protestantism is often associated with optimism—an optimism that the tragedy of the war might have overturned but which instead proved resilient. But optimism did not necessarily permeate the culture at all levels. In his *Popular Mood of Pre-Civil War America,* Lewis O. Saum argues that the common American temperament was "abiding moroseness." If optimism was not widespread, if Americans were more pessimistic than is sometimes realized, the "popular mood" would have been less vulnerable to the war. In any case, Saum demonstrates a cultural acceptance of death as an event to be endured with religious resignation. Saum also contends that the common American view of life was providential. "Simply put, that view held that, directly or indirectly, God controlled all things." Certainly, many soldiers entered the war with a providential view of the world. For them, their wartime experiences only increased the extent to which they attributed the world's happenings to Providence. To be sure, rebellion was a product of will, and it was rebellion which inspired Confederates to become soldiers and shoot Union men. But in battle itself intentional actions struck one less than randomness. At the 123rd New York Volunteer Infantry's first battle, "without the usual skirmishing that would have warned us to lie down, a volley was fired from the enemy's line and bullets began to whistle and sing." Rice C. Bull stood next to Jerry Finch. "At the first round Jerry's gun tumbled from his hands and he staggered and fell at my feet." That evening, Bull found that a bullet had hit the stock of his gun and another had gone through his coffee pail. That was the nature of battle: one man was shot; the other, standing next to him, spared. While the soldier quickly learned caution and care in battle, he was all too aware that he could not prevent his own death. Death came to whom it would. Sometimes it seemed accidental. But the soldier preferred to think of death in battle as providential. If human actions did not determine who lived and who died—if one's own personal actions did not control the result—then divine will did. And if this seemed true in battle, what about disease, the far greater killer of the war? Almost all soldiers got sick; the same disease would kill one man while the other recovered. Once again, maintaining the prewar understanding of Providence served as the best explanation.[6]

Martha V. Pike and Janice Gray Armstrong observe that "in the nineteenth and the preceding centuries, death was often sudden, but never unexpected." Death was not only ubiquitous—it always will be—but it was public. People, if lucky, died in their own homes. Infant mortality and death in childbirth were common enough that the roots of death in life itself were plain to see. While the war may have increased Christians' awareness of death, such awareness was already enjoined on them. Perhaps it was Burt's death that made Laforest Dunham recognize the nearness of death. He wrote home that "Iff thare is any place that a person ought to lade a criston life heare is the place, for a person dont know what time he will be cald up for to leave this world of trouble." The link he made between "a criston life" and the realization that death may come at any time, however, was one he might have made without any war at all. Laforest went on to portray death conventionally as a deliverance and heaven as a reunited home. "Iff it should be my lot to fall, I hope and trust that we will all meat in a better world whare wore and troubles are know more."[7]

Nurse Emily Parsons said of patients who had died that they had *gone home;* "They seemed willing to go." Phillip Shaw Paludan points out that during the years after the war— which had brought death to "at least a quarter of a million Northern households"—a new obsession with the afterlife emerged. A new demand arose for books describing the after-life, books which allowed those grieving to imagine where the dead soldiers had gone. The newly imagined heaven turned out to look very much like the idealized Victorian home. Americans could anticipate death as the means to be reunited with their loved ones; heaven was conceived of as a place where friends and family resume their social intercourse. "But you loved ones who do miss us, do not miss us with any degree of regret, but think of us as those who have gone forth to battle for you and our liberty and should we fall then console your thoughts by ever traveling toward that Home where parting will be no more"—this was one soldier's advice to those left behind. In heaven, if not on earth, the vacant chair would once again be filled.[8]

Daniel Faust wrote his mother, saying, "I think the lord will keep me safe to come home again and if not I hope we all meet in heaven where there will be no war any more where the rebells against heaven will haf to stay in the forts of punishment, where they cant part us anymore." The contemporary song "Comrades, I Am Dying" portrayed a "sick and wounded" soldier on the battlefield who sees his mother "coming down from heaven" to "teach him how to die" and to bear his soul back to God. The alternatives American culture offered the northern soldier, if the soldier believed, were happy ones. If he lived, he could return home to his family. If he died, he could meet them in a heaven very much like home. This potent mixture of heaven and home inspired the believer to persevere in his service to God, family, and country; unfortunately, it inspired the believer on the Confederate side fully as well. It also inspired black soldiers. One of the favorite songs among the black soldiers at Beaufort, South Carolina, was "I Can't Stay Behind." It said, "My father is gone into heaven, my Lord! I can't stay behind!" and promised that there is "Room enough in heaven for de sojer."[9]

Americans hoped that they and their loved ones would make "good deaths." This is why Laforest Dunham carefully told his family that Albertus had requested that the Bible be read to him. Even though Albertus was not always in his right mind, he was—as they would have said at the time— "sensible" of the fact he was dying. Lewis O. Saum has demonstrated the centrality of the deathbed to mid–nineteenth-century culture. There gathered family, friends, and even strangers to observe the death. They hoped to provide "solicitude, emotional comfort, and some reassurance for the departing," while "receiving inspiration by witnessing a calm and clear-eyed death." They also enjoyed a "guarded hope for the soul of the deceased that derived from a demonstration of Christian fortitude and resignation." "To die" was an active, not a passive, verb. Conversely, "an unattended death sparked terror and signified a great spiritual and emotional loss."[10]

Many deaths, of course, went unattended before and after the Civil War. But the relentless carnage in the hospital and on the battlefield during the war meant a massive wave of unattended deaths which might create "terror" and "a great spiritual and emotional loss." On the one hand, it was almost impossible for a man to make a "good death" on the battlefield. On the other hand, all battlefield deaths, all military deaths except those by execution, could be made into "good deaths." In the Gettysburg Address, when Lincoln spoke of the deaths that had consecrated that field, he hardly had to inquire into the nature of any individual death. Each one had been a good death, because every soldier had died for the Union. If relations and loved ones sought reassurance that the departed had died well, the war for the Union offered them that reassurance more firmly than did peacetime. In *Miss Ravenel's Conversion from Secession to Loyalty,* Captain Colburne listened to the pitiful and horrible sounds of wounded men dying as they were being transported from Port Hudson to New Orleans. "All these men, thought Colburne, are dying and agonizing for their country and for human freedom." Colburne was wounded himself. "He prayed, and without arguing the matter, he wearily yet calmly trusted that God would grant them His infinite mercy in this world and the other." Perhaps this confidence is why it appeared to an unhappy Presbyterian like Reuben Smith Goodman that among the sick, wounded, and dying "the majority are trusting more in their own righteousness than in Christ."[11]

More than that, the war for the Union offered more meaning for death than it may have had in peacetime. George W. Crosley described his feelings during the battle of Shiloh. "Death had no terrors for me then for I knew that I was in the performance of the noblest duty—except the worship of God that a man is ever permitted to perform here upon earth." The duty was risking one's life to preserve country, and killing people, which was merely incidental to the duty. Compared with the deaths that stemmed from fulfilling this duty, how meaningful were most deaths in peacetime?[12]

Samuel Storrow assured his parents that "Death isn't the end of *every*thing." That was a comfort. One reason death did not end everything was that the dead themselves made demands. Storrow was certain that the dead Union soldiers themselves, the spirits of those who had died in this great war, insisted that those who lived continue to fight. In a sense, the dead called for more dead. Storrow, like other northern soldiers, believed that those who already died in service had created an unavoidable duty for the living.[13]

Americans thought of the nation as a community of the living and dead. The American family extended in time. The dead remained part of the American nation; they still made claims upon the living and they could still find fulfillment in the nation's destiny. Northerners had gone to war to preserve the nation left them by the Revolutionary generation, meeting an obligation they felt toward that generation. By the time of the Gettysburg Address, northerners added the Union dead to those whose deaths made them moral obligees of the living. Lincoln, articulating the deeply felt sense of many northerners, vowed that "these dead shall not have died in vain." "It is for us the living, rather, to be dedicated here to the unfinished work which they who fought here have thus so far nobly advanced." Their deaths had sealed that obligation. To give those deaths meaning, Lincoln promised more war, more dying. Only by prosecuting the war, rather than negotiating a peace, could Union victory and "a new birth of freedom" be guaranteed. All Union deaths were good deaths; furthermore all Union deaths had a good cause.

Indeed, for the Civil War generation the cultural problem

poised by the massive carnage of the war may have had less to do with death than it did with mourning. The nineteenth century had turned grief into an art; as Pike and Armstrong say in *A Time to Mourn,* "Nineteenth Century Americans mourned well." Grief had an elaborate etiquette, with its own costumes, behavior, and ritual, all socially prescribed. Families in the North could follow these rituals even in the face of widespread death, and many of them did so. Within the army itself, there was barely time to acknowledge individual deaths, let alone to show the proper respect to the dead—the burial of Albertus Dunham was exceptional. So was the imaginary burial portrayed in Mrs. E. A. B. Mitchell's "Bear Gently, So Gently the Roughly Made Bier," a "touching ballad" whose popularity attests to civilian fantasies of sentimental rituals of death within the army. And even while civilians might have time to mourn their own dead, how could they mourn all the dead created by this war? In light of this, it is not surprising that the postwar years saw such relentless monumentalization of the war—with cemeteries as the first form of memorialization—or that the war's most cherished utterance came at the dedication of a graveyard. The generations of Americans that later recited Lincoln's Gettysburg Address were finally paying the Union dead their ritualistic due.[14]

Nineteenth-century Americans, even soldiers at war, enjoyed cemeteries. Ira Pettit spent an afternoon browsing among the graves in an Alexandria churchyard. Inscriptions which particularly interested him he copied down and sent to his sister. Sergeant Lavalette Griffin sent his sister praise of the cemetery in Pensacola, Florida: "It is filled with shade trees not like our northern graveyards laid out in straight rows at equal distance, but left to grow promiscuously as nature intended. The greater proportion of the graves are old Spanish tombs, but there are some of the most splendid monuments of modern date that I ever saw. It is mostly fenced off in lots with brick or iron fences. All kinds of flowers abound, a good share of which are in bloom." He also found the ages listed on the tombstones reassuringly high, which he took as evidence Pensacola was healthy. Corporal Lawrence Van Alstyne admired Louden Park Cemetery in Maryland—"Shade trees all over it, great fine monuments, and vaults as large as small houses"—he concluded "Only rich people are buried there."[15]

Northern culture developed another justification for the soldier's death, although it was one rarely shared by soldiers themselves and perhaps not widely accepted at all. It was an interpretation, however, that was expressed in much of the literate culture of the time and one that has come down to us in one of the era's more powerful songs, "The Battle Hymn of the Republic." This interpretation presents the death of the Union soldier as something analogous to the death of Christ—indeed, while it is strongly rooted in nineteenth-century Protestantism, it is almost blasphemous in its equation of the soldier with Christ.

Julia Ward Howe, who wrote the words for "The Battle Hymn of the Republic," was a New England woman of abolitionist sentiment. (After the war, she also became one of the first proponents of "Mother's Day.") When the war against slavery joined the war for the Union, Howe successfully combined Christian fervor and war-making. Union soldiers became agents of divine will. She persuaded many northern soldiers to sing:

> As He died to make men holy
> Let us die to make men free.

Julia Ward Howe wrote the battle hymn before the killing got serious. The image of the soldier as Christ comes from the hospital, where nurses could see the soldiers' experience overwhelmingly in terms of their suffering. Hannah Ropes went as far as confessing that "I like the patients very much better before they are able to be dressed and walk out"—once mobile, even wounded soldiers tended to indulge in tobacco and alcohol.[16] The image of the soldier as Christ worked less well in camp—too much activity and too much sinfulness—and on the battlefield not at all. The image of the soldier as Christ does not allow the fact that the soldier's fundamental duty is not to suffer but to kill. If I rewrite "The Battle Hymn of the Republic"—a battle hymn that deals remarkably little with battle—the point becomes clear:

> As He killed to make men holy
> Let us kill to make them free.

That image would never do. In this battle hymn, the fighting is done by the Lord, not by the soldiers. The soldiers' part is to worship and to die.

A troubling image, full of contradictions. Portraying the soldier as Christ emphasized his suffering. This portrayal was one way to do justice to the depth of individual suffering and the large-scale extent of sickness and death. It also offered tautological reassurance of the legitimacy of the Union cause and the meaningfulness of Union deaths—a cause that the Christlike soldier would die for was manifestly a holy one and one worth dying for. The death of the soldier justified the death of the soldier. Finally, the image of the Christlike soldier obliterated the transformation of the plain citizen into a killer. Too much attention to the horrors that northern soldiers inflicted would have raised questions about their reintegration into postwar society. People back home preferred to believe that war ennobled men.[17]

Katharine Wormeley, aboard a hospital ship during the Peninsula Campaign, said of the sick men, "Instances of such high unselfishness happen daily that, though I forget them daily, I feel myself strengthened in my trust of human nature."

She and other nurses told stories of sick or wounded men insisting that others be attended first, of men bearing pain, crippling, and death stoicly, even cheerfully, of men maintaining their belief in the justice of the Union cause until the end. Julia S. Wheelock's *The Boys in White; The Experience of a Hospital Agent in and around Washington,* a postwar memoir, was devoted not to tales of recovery but tales of death. "The boys in white" was her phrase for those "boys in blue" who died. She assumed that in death they all donned angelic robes. Her words on the hospital death of her brother, Oliver Wheelock, convey something of the tone of the whole book. "But to the dying saint death had no terror, for 'his anchor was cast within the veil,' and 'that anchor holds.'" The doctrine of resurrection was her comfort, and she believed the comfort of thousands of grieving northern women. The soldiers "will rise to enjoy all that angels feel of the celestial love and peace, to swell the anthem of the redeemed, which, beginning upon the outer ranks of the hosts of God, rolls inward, growing deeper and louder until it gathers and breaks in one full deep symphony of praise around the throne."[18]

Indeed, some people hoped for a redemptive quality in the blood of the Union soldier. After seeing the wounded from the battle of the Wilderness in May 1864, one woman wrote, "Oh, if this baptism of blood does not purify this country and cleanse it of greed and selfish ambitions as well as of slavery, then the nation will deserve to become extinct."[19] Henry Grimes Marshall, an officer in a black regiment, argued that the war had purified the country, partly by killing. "God has come nearer to many families by taking some member who has gone forth to fight for their country and has not it been good for them." Death, he believed, was bringing northern families to God—as was fear of death. "And don't all those who have friends in the Army have something definite to pray for and their formality drops off." Because of this, Marshall concluded that a "more earnest manly piety and practical Christianity pervades the church and the masses of the people." Yet in October 1865, looking at the war's influence on himself, he had to acknowledge that the "life in the Army has, in one sense, demoralized me and I don't feel like the same man as when I entered the service." Marshall wanted to be a minister and yet found himself uninterested in other individuals and unable to reach out to them.[20]

Even though he too believed in the redemptive nature of the war, Marshall's picture of men demoralized by war hardly seemed Christlike. Outside of the army it was easier to portray the soldiers as redeemers. In 1876, Mrs. C. E. McKay instructed northerners that the soldiers who had died were "not behind the martyrs of olden time in courage on the battle-field, patience and self-renunciation in fulfilling the new and hard duties of a soldier's life, fortitude under suffering, meekness and submission in the hour of death." She had been a nurse in the hospitals, where "the true spirit of the Christian martyr arose triumphant and faced, without blenching, the last enemy." She had watched many men die. One of them spoke to her the instant before he died. "I want to tell you—what— what I will do for you—when I get to another place—" This dying man—presumably Catholic—could already think of himself as given the powers of intercession. She called upon northerners to remember "the bodily pains and perils, the mental anguish and bloody deaths, through which these grand souls wrought out for us a new national life." Mrs. McKay sought reassurance for a personal grief—her brother, shot through the chest, died at Chancellorsville.[21]

When Hannah Ropes described one soldier's death, she confused his temporal home with his eternal one. "The nurse came and asked me to go in and see Powers; he lay sleeping quietly under cover of which the angels were loosing him from the clay prison, the hospital life so painfully distasteful to him, and making ready for him a home for which he pined in silence, for which he was so eminently fitted." To Ropes, the home for which Powers was "eminently fitted" was his heavenly one, and she hoped that progressive diminishment was preparing him for death. But it was unlikely that it was the home "for which he pined in silence" and Ropes knew this. Powers probably longed for his home here on earth. "I was glad he was unconscious," Ropes said, "for he had a wife and two pretty children; their likeness lay under the pillow where his head rested, with the death damp dripping like tears unto the case so precious to him!" Powers' wife had surely fulfilled the duties of true womanhood for this soldier, her husband, about whom everything "betokened respectability of soul and life." "Above his head was his Bible, presented by his wife, with her name on the flyleaf." Hannah Ropes offered Powers as an image of the good man. Even on his deathbed, this northern soldier united the cherished themes of patriotism, Christianity, and domesticity. In celebrating this constellation of values, Hannah Ropes was not alone.[22]

When John Ryder, the son of Mercy Jenkins Ryder, was wounded at Kennesaw Mountain, he believed that he was dying—indeed, he had "always expected I should be killed before the war would be over." But on April 7, 1864, his twenty-first birthday, he had publicly confessed his Christian faith; now, lying on the field and waiting for death, he was reconciled. He thought, "I am glad I settled this matter last winter between myself and God, and now I am sure I shall sometime meet Mother in Heaven."[23]

Afterword
The Soldiers' War:
The Junction of Social History
and Military History

> I believe if there is anybody in the world that fulfills the
> Apostle's injunction, "beareth all things," and "endureth
> all things," it is the soldier.
>
> *Wilbur Fisk*[1]

Commitment, Mobilization, Cohesion

Presenting the northern soldier as the embodiment of Christian disciplehood, Wilbur Fisk deftly combined religion, patriotism, and the war experience in much the way that Hannah Ropes illuminated the deathbed of the soldier Powers. But Fisk made more immediate military claims for the northern soldier than did Ropes. Fisk also argued, during the war itself, that the nation's ultimate victory depended on the soldier. In

April 1864, as the Army of the Potomac prepared for the bloody Wilderness campaign, Fisk wrote home that in this rebellion "the people have not rebelled against the few, but the few have rebelled against the people." The "proud slave-holder" wished to destroy the government of the people and create a new nation built on slavery. Could the slaveholders' rebellion succeed? Fisk asserted that "If the North will do her duty, we answer, Never! And the North *will* do her duty." The North would destroy the Confederate armies, the Confederate government, and the Confederate institution of slavery. Wilbur Fisk was sure of ultimate Union victory because he was sure of the perseverance of the northern soldier. "Never in a war before did the rank and file feel a more resolute earnestness for a just cause, and more invincible determination to succeed, than in this war; and what the rank and file are determined to do everybody knows will be done."[2]

The claims that Wilbur Fisk made for northern soldiers— their commitment to the Union and the necessity of that commitment for Union victory—points us to one of the places where military history, political history, and social history all join. The military historian might address soldiers' perseverance as a matter of mobilization and cohesion; the political historian as a matter of ideology and political culture; the social historian as an issue of class or culture. Clearly, the question "Why do men fight?" must be addressed if the Civil War is to be understood. And the question must also be refined, so that instead of being directed toward some innate male characteristic, it focuses on certain men from a specific culture fighting their peculiar war. "Why did Americans of the 1860s fight?" Here the social historian can offer insights that will be useful to the military historian.

The military historian, in turn, can furnish material and concepts to the social historian. Small-unit cohesion, for example, a theory of military sociologists, can help reveal what happened to the northern volunteers after they arrived at the front.

The history of technology, tactics, strategy, and what is sometimes called "modern war" or "total war" can help explain why the war became a bloodbath—and why it became an assault on the southern social order. And the historian of domesticity, in its southern form, might well consult with the historian of war to consider the way in which the Civil War's impact on the southern homefront was crucial to Union victory. (One does not know, however, whether to say these historians should "join forces" or arrange a marriage, if only of convenience.)[3]

We must avoid treating the northern will to fight, in 1861 or in 1864, as foreordained. The formation and cohesion of armies—getting what Napoleon called the heaviest battalions into the field and keeping them there—were crucial to Union victory. What would have happened if the people of the Union had not supported the war? Specifically, what would have happened if the men of the North had not volunteered in droves in 1861? And what would have happened if the veteran soldiers had not reenlisted in 1864—as more than half did? The answer is that despite the material superiority that the Union possessed there would have been no war at all— Confederate independence would have been a fact.

The way in which localities and states raised the troops is sometimes treated as an unfortunate concession to localism. In the absence of a federal apparatus for raising large numbers of men and of any national tradition for such a procedure, the federal government probably could not have mobilized the armies directly. Statewide mobilization was hardly a concession to localism; it was a necessity. The federal government was dependent on the states. Many Americans had dealt with no other United States official than the local postmaster.[4]

When Lincoln issued his first call for troops in April 1861, he acted not from the constitutional right to raise armies—a right limited to Congress in any case—but from a statute that permitted him to order out the various state militia. While the federal government seemed to dither in indecision, the state governors enlisted more soldiers than the War Department knew what to do with. Arguably, what saved Washington, D.C., itself, in its isolation in the first weeks of the war, was not any energy or decision on the part of the federal government but the speed and vigor with which Massachusetts governor John Andrew raised and organized troops, the characteristic decisiveness and uncharacteristic military competence of Massachusetts militia general Benjamin F. Butler, and the initiative and hustle of the northern volunteer soldier.[5]

Why did these men of 1861 rush into the armies? Why were they so eager that the War Department could not keep up with the enlistments and that various northern states complained that other states were being allowed to contribute more soldiers than they were? There are many reasons that men enlisted—youthful high spirits, community pressure, the overpowering enthusiasm. But the volunteers of 1861, who continued to compose the bulk of the Union army throughout the war, were motivated by ideology as well. Apparently, Republican Mothers had done their job well.

The principal incentive that volunteers shared was their love for the Union. To them, the Union meant both the ideals of liberty and democracy that they believed unique to the United States, and the government that would uphold those ideals. They agreed with Abraham Lincoln that secession, by threatening to tear down the only government based on these ideals, threatened to destroy the ideals themselves. They also felt that the Union was a precious legacy, handed down to them by the Revolutionary fathers. Defending it was in many ways a familial duty, something that a son owed the generations before him. In February 1862, Private Wilbur Fisk, testified to the emotional strength of the ideology of Union. On night-time picket in northern Virginia, the soldiers marveled at their position. "When we reflect that we are standing on the outer verge of all that is left of the American Union, and nothing but darkness and rebellion is beyond, and that we are actually guarding our own homes and firesides from treason's usurpations, we feel a thrill of pride that we are permitted to bear a part in maintaining our beloved Government." The Union was a man's family writ large.[6]

In a war where men enlisted for a confusing multiplicity of terms—three-month enlistments, nine-month enlistments, one-, two-, and three-year enlistments—getting men into the army did not guarantee keeping them in the army for the duration. That was a problem that would particularly concern the Lincoln administration during the winter of 1863–64. Another question was more immediate in 1861–62. "How would the Union use its power to defeat the Confederacy?" That question proved difficult for the Union to answer and out-and-out impossible for many of the leading commanders, most notably George McClellan. The innovations in military technology that marked the Civil War were not matched by a comparable innovations in tactical thinking. Successfully applying the superior force that the Union possessed seemed impossible for Union generals.

George McClellan at least had strategic brilliance on his side. His Peninsula campaign certainly should have worked; the demonstrable fact that George McClellan was gutless should not discredit his plan. As a result of Seven Pines and the Seven Days, the Confederate army defending Richmond lost more than 26,000 men—nearly 30 percent of its available forces. The Army of the Potomac lost slightly more than 20,000, only about 20 percent of their forces. The strategy of taking up a position where the Confederates had to launch frontal assaults was justified—or would have been if McClellan had not panicked and retreated.

After McClellan, Union generals in the East favored "the direct approach"—march overland to Richmond, seeking a decisive battle that would destroy Lee's army. But if McClellan showed that brains were not enough, Hooker and

Burnside showed that guts alone were insufficient—or at least not the kind of moral courage that could commit troops to one battle in the hopes that one battle was all it took to win the war. These generals were unable to see what to do after a defeat—which makes one wonder if they would have known what to do after a victory. Thus Pope was defeated at Second Bull Run; McClellan was immobilized by victory at Antietam; Burnside and Hooker were immobilized by their defeats at Fredericksburg, and at Chancellorsville; and Meade had little idea what to do with his victory at Gettysburg. In fact, the Union fundamentally decided to have its principal army, the Army of the Potomac, act as a shield against Lee's army, while its armies in the West won campaigns and conquered territory.

Until Grant came east. Grant recognized the material basis of Union superiority, and planned to bring "the heaviest battalions" into play methodically. His was a strategy not of battles or campaigns but of war. Russell Weigley said of Grant, "He developed a highly uncommon ability to rise above the fortunes of a single battle and to master the flow of a long series of events, almost to the point of making any outcome of a single battle, victory, draw, or even defeat, serve his eventual purpose equally well."[7]

Grant believed in hitting the principal Confederate armies with concentrated forces. Because of the Union's material base, he could do this. He also believed that the way to apply this superior force was to fight every day in every theater of the war. Under his direction in 1864, all Union armies began an advance, eliminating the Confederacy's earlier advantage of using interior lines to shift troops around to where the threat was greatest. As Lincoln told him and he told his commanders, "Those not skinning can hold a leg."[8] This was a war of annihilation based on the recognition that to beat the Confederacy, its armies must be destroyed. Grant's army was the point of the spear, and behind it was the weight of superior northern population, industrial base, agricultural production, wealth.

It worked, but the human cost was immense. In fact, the human cost was so great that it threatened to undermine the military strategy, because it threatened to sicken the northern people to the point they would have been unwilling to continue the war. Yankee private Wilbur Fisk had his tongue carefully placed in his cheek when he said, "The more we get used to being killed, the better we like it."[9] Consider the casualties that earned Grant his reputation as butcher. During the first month of the 1864 campaign, as the Army of the Potomac ground its way from the Rapidan through the Wilderness to the nightmare of Cold Harbor, it suffered approximately 55,000 casualties—about the total strength of the Army of Northern Virginia at the start of the campaign. In the process, it inflicted 32,000 casualties—a ratio of roughly 5 to 3, which is higher than the 5 to 2 superiority that the Union possessed over the Confederacy, and is not an unreasonable proportion considering the advantages that the defense had in Civil War battles.[10]

Still, it is a little glib, even cold-blooded, to say that these are reasonable casualties. They are certainly higher in proportion to population than the United States would accept today. So we must remember the material and ideological bases of Union superiority. First, as high as this proportion was, it was lower than what the Confederacy suffered. Second, the northern people believed that saving the Union was worth it, certainly more than the American people thought victory in Vietnam was worth its casualties, and more than Confederates thought that independent nationhood was worth the casualties Grant's armies were inflicting. Nonetheless, it was a near thing. If Sherman had not captured Atlanta on the eve of the 1864 presidential election, it is possible that Lincoln and the pro-war party would have been defeated.

The soldiers' ideology continued to motivate them through the hellish second half of the war. Furthermore, by the middle of the war, many soldiers had developed even stronger loyalties to keep them in the army. These were loyalties to their fellow soldiers, specifically to the men they served with in their messes, companies, and regiments. The jargon that military thinkers use to indicate this kind of loyalty is small-unit cohesion. All armies at all times count on it. Added to the ideology of 1861, the small-unit cohesion of 1864 created the tenacity that kept soldiers in the army so that the Union could keep an army in the field.

Perhaps the best way to understand small-unit cohesion is to think of the company as a substitute family. That, at least, is how the soldiers themselves came to feel about it. Corporal Lawrence Van Alstyne, for example, referred to the himself and the three men who shared his tent as "our family." The months of service that turned volunteers into veterans also created in them dependence on their fellow veterans, indeed even a love—any other word would be inadequate—for their fellow soldiers. Leaving the army meant leaving behind men with whom one had served, suffered, and risked one's life. The affections of this substitute family competed with the claims of the family a soldier had left at home.[11]

The loyalty the soldiers displayed extended beyond that owed to the living. As befitted "a nation founded in blood," soldiers felt bound to the dead as well—to, in Lincoln's phrase in his First Inaugural, "every patriot grave." Specifically, they feel obliged to those men who had served by their sides and were now gone, having died in the hospital or battlefield or having been sent home wounded, some of them maimed for life. Like their own families, or the perpetual Union they fought to preserve, their military families included the living and the dead. Abandoning the war meant making a mockery of their sacrifices.[12]

In the winter of 1863–64, the Union government made

every appeal—and used every bribe—it could think of to persuade soldiers already in the army to reenlist. These were the
best soldiers the Union had, impossible to replace and just as
impossible to keep against their wills. Without them, there
would be no spring campaign in 1864. There was none of the
naive enthusiasm of 1861 to call on; these men had lost any
illusions about war. Over half of them reenlisted. "There is
much talk of reenlisting again," Frederick Pettit wrote home
in December 1863. "I think a number of our regiment will
reenlist. This shows perhaps our opinion of the war better than
I can express it."[13]

That in itself suggested the commitment of the rank-and-
file to the cause of the Union, but as a sign of this commitment it
was surpassed by the soldiers' vote in the fall elections. This
reenlistment was crucial for army cohesion, but it took place
before the bloody spring campaigns, with the heavy loss in life,
the failed and sometimes senseless frontal assaults that eventually led to soldiers displaying a Cold Harbor syndrome and
officers complaining that the men would not press attacks
home. Still, even after the dreadful summer campaigns in
Virginia, where the armies invented modern trench warfare
around Petersburg, the soldiers of the Union voted overwhelming for Abraham Lincoln and the Republican party in the 1864
election—voted, indeed, for the continuance of the war.[14]

How did the Union succeed in employing its heaviest
battalions? The Union succeeded because the men who made
up those battalions volunteered to be employed, not just in
1861, when they might not have known better, but in 1864 as
well. Understanding why these men continued to risk their
lives requires considering a great many factors, some of them
not commonly associated with military analysis. Some of these
factors—the ones I have called "domestic imagery"—have
been considered in preceding chapters. Before concluding this
discussion of military victory and defeat, we might judge the
importance of domesticity to the Confederacy. What did it

mean when northern soldiers found the will to extend the war
to women and children, to make war upon the homes of their
enemies?

Domesticity and Confederate Defeat

The Confederate armies were also built on volunteers. The
experience of fighting together should have created the same
small unit loyalties in the Confederate army, and in fact it did
create the same loyalties. Nonetheless, by the end of the war,
the Confederate armies were dissolving. By the spring of 1865,
lack of men wrecked the Confederate war effort. Even though
all the factors that created cohesion within the Union army
operated as thoroughly on the Confederate army, the will to
make war was crippled by the obligations men felt to their
families.

In April 1865, Robert E. Lee attributed the defeat of the
Army of Northern Virginia—which immediately led to the
surrender of all Confederate armies—to its "moral condition."
"The operations which occurred while the troops were in the
entrenchments in front of Richmond and Petersburg were not
marked by the boldness and decision which formerly characterized them." What caused this moral condition was "the state
of feeling in the country," and particularly, "the communica-
tions received by the men from their homes, urging their return and the abandonment of the field." "From what I have
seen and learned, I believe an army cannot be organized or
supported in Virginia, and as far as I know the condition of
affairs, the country east of the Mississippi is morally and physically unable to maintain the contest." And a less well known
soldier, Charles Fenton James, wrote his sister in February
1865 about how soldiers, listening to "the voice of despon-

dency," started to desert. "The only fear that I ever felt was that the spirit of the people and the army might flag."[15]

Why did the soldiers go home in 1865? One reason that Confederate soldiers became demoralized was death—death in the camp and hospital, death on the battlefield, death in defeat and even death in glorious victory. The surest way to demoralize a man is to kill him. And a lot of men went home in the spring of 1865 because they foresaw the inevitability of defeat and failed to see any reason to wait around and be killed. Low rations made men fear for their health and doubt the ability of the Confederate government to survive. One North Carolina soldier considered deserting because the prospects for victory were so slim; he wrote his wife to "tell the children that I cant come to see them unless I runaway." Another soldier wrote, "I am tired of so much fiting for they is some part of the permotac army most allers afiting." He was war-weary—"I am tired of hering guns let alone fiting"—and he worried for his family. "My little boy was sick and Eliza was give out wek with the rumitiz." Perhaps the most important reasons for Confederate desertion was the tug of home.[16]

"I want you to come home as soon as you can after you get this letter." This plaintive cry of a Confederate woman moves us well over a hundred years after she wrote it; imagine its impact on her husband. Indeed, some diehard Confederates began blaming southern women for men's desertion. "Where is the virtuous woman of the eighteenth century?" lamented Buck Long. "Oh! that she was still in our land to scorn and drive from door to door the cowardly deserter." Charles Fenton James told his sister, "Desertion takes place because desertion is encouraged, because the name deserter has ceased, in a great measure, to be a reproach and disgrace." It was the women who should make it a disgrace: "The women of the Confederacy have the power, if they have the will and determination, to save the country." The Reverend John Paris, who preached a sermon—and then published it—at the mass execution of twenty-two deserters, said that most of the men executed had been persuaded to desert by an "appeal from home." After the war one of Lee's staff officers, Walter H. Taylor, confessed that, during the last months of the fighting, "hundreds of letters addressed to soldiers were intercepted and sent to army headquarters, in which mothers, wives and sisters, told of their inability to respond to the appeals of hungry children for bread, or to provide proper care and remedies for the sick; and in the name of all that was dear, appealed to the men to come home and rescue them from the ills which they suffered and the starvation that threatened them." Apparently Confederate wives were finally acting the way that the author of "A Few Words in Behalf of the Loyal Women of the United States by One of Themselves" had wanted them to act. Instead of being the voice of passionate rebellion, they spoke for resignation and reason.[17]

Confederate soldiers left their wives—and their mothers, sweethearts, daughters, fathers, sons, family, and friends—at higher risk than most Union soldiers left theirs. And as the war went on, the dangers that the people back home faced grew more widespread. Confederate soldiers found themselves torn between two duties, one to the Confederacy, one to their families. After 1864, some Confederates saw the war as likely to end in defeat; others saw it as unlikely to end at all. Not surprisingly, more of them chose their duty to their families over their duty to the Confederacy, even over their duty to their fellow soldiers.

To a large degree, the dangers that called the soldiers home came from the fact of war itself. Food was in all too short supply throughout the Confederacy. Inflation made Confederate money almost worthless—and the soldiers were paid so little to begin with. Clothes, when available, were expensive; medicine was unaffordable. Most of the grown men—the grown white men—were in the army and left the burden of farming and other work to women, the young, and the elderly. The people of the South faced a very real danger of malnutrition, even starvation. The toll the war took on the health of the non-combatant has never been successfully measured, but it must have been immense.

Other fears came directly from the Union army. As the federal troops headed south, particularly as Sherman marched through Georgia, Confederates recognized the prospect that those they left at home would soon find Yankee soldiers on their streets, in their farmyards, and even inside their houses. The Union army was an army of invasion, seemingly irresistible everywhere except the territory just north of Richmond. How could a man protect his family when he was hundreds of miles away?

Sergeant Edwin H. Fay told his wife, "If you desire it, dearest one, I will come home at any cost, for I hold my first duty is to my family, my country is secondary." Indeed, his correspondence sometimes seemed intended to raise in her the fears that would lead her to call him back home. When Union forces began operating in the vicinity of Minden, Louisiana, his hometown, he advised her to wear a pistol at all times; if a Yankee insulted her, "blow his brains out." He wrote her the story of Yankees trapping two ladies in their parlor and then raping two slave women to death before their eyes. Sergeant Fay's wife never did instruct him to desert—perhaps to his disappointment.[18]

William L. Nugent was initially optimistic about the impact of Union occupation, assuring his wife "I judge you will not be in any danger at home." The Yankees would compel her to give up her slaves, but they would also "compel them to obey & respect you." But soon he advised her to leave her home, if the Union forces set up a contraband camp in the vicinity—"anything but being kept in close proximity to a camp of demoralized negroes."[19]

The women and children left behind faced more than

hard times and the threat of Union armies. They faced the increasingly sure destruction of slavery; they lived among a people newly free. Southern institutions of racial oppression had been rationalized as necessary means to control a savage people. Now the men who had been the force behind the laws of slave control were in the army, far from their homes.

Slavery, said Alexander H. Stephens in his most quoted line, was the cornerstone of the Confederacy. It was the institution that the Confederacy had been created to protect; in turn, some southerners argued that it was the institution that would protect the Confederacy. The Confederacy could field such a high proportion of its white men precisely because loyal black men and women could be expected to perform the other labor necessary for the South to function, only because the slaves were contented and would not rebel.

And yet . . . and yet. The Old South had been fiercely afraid of slave rebellion, rebellion that might fall most heavily on women and children. And wartime slave management was not simply a concern but a matter of policy: the so-called "twenty nigger law," that exempted those men who owned or oversaw twenty or more slaves from the draft, was designed to ensure effective plantation management. While slavery supposedly freed up white men to fight Yankees, slavery also required enough white men left behind to see that the slaves did not free themselves.

The fact was, however, that the number of strong, active white men left behind to manage the plantation economy, govern the slaves, and protect white women was inadequate. Slave management was a burden that fell increasingly on women. The assurances of slave faithfulness and of black docility were never more needed. And they had never been harder to believe. Masters learned that slaves had never loved slavery. One soldier, for example, received a letter from his wife "stating that his Negroes were killing up his hogs, dogs, chickens, & c. and cutting up generally." Soldiers learned of incidents of violence, black against white; they feared for their families in a countryside filled with Yankees and newly freed black people; even the calmest white people acknowledged a rising level of independence and assertiveness among black people—they called it insubordination, ingratitude, and sauciness.[20]

These were the factors that undermined the cohesion of the Confederate army—not simply death and defeat but the fears men had that their families would be crushed as traditional southern society came crashing down around them. The men who answered their wives' calls and went home were hardly cowards, nor were the realists who saw the handwriting on the wall. Their good sense took away from Jefferson Davis and Robert E. Lee the means of prosecuting the war. The point must be made—had the Confederate soldiery remained in the field, the war would have continued, and almost certainly would have grown in brutality. And had that soldiery not gone home but headed to the hills to pursue guerrilla warfare, the war could have dragged on indefinitely—and the Confederate soldier would have come home to no home at all. If the Union army's cohesion made Union victory possible, lack of cohesion accounted for the timing of Confederate defeat. In December 1864, Lincoln spoke of the Confederate president Jefferson Davis, saying, "Between him and us the issue is distinct, simple, and inflexible. It is an issue which can only be tried by war, and decided by victory." Lincoln cast the prospect of victory and defeat as a matter of Union and Confederate will. "If we yield we are beaten; if the Southern people fail him, he is beaten."[21]

Lincoln's December 1864 message to Congress came after the Union army had taken Atlanta and after Union voters, including the rank and file of the army, had elected him to another four years in office. He used the message to boast of the vitality of the Union, seemingly stronger after four years of war. He pointed out "that we have more men now than we had when the war began; that we are not exhausted, nor in the process of exhaustion." The Union could "maintain the contest indefinitely." In manpower and in the other materials of war, the Union still had the heaviest battalions. More important, "the public purpose to reestablish and maintain the national authority is unchanged, and, as we believed, unchangeable." Without that resolution, the heaviest battalions could not have been brought into play. That resolution was the cause of Union victory and Confederate defeat in 1865. In turn, northern conceptions of manhood, familial duties, and the home helped maintain the resolution of the northern soldiers. The northern soldier did not simply experience the war as a husband, son, father, or brother—he fought it that way as well. That was part of his strength. The Confederate soldier fought the war the same way, and, in the end, that proved part of his weakness.

Notes

Introduction

1. John J. Ryder, *Reminiscences of Three Years' Service in the Civil War: By a Cape Cod Boy* (New Bedford, Mass., 1928), 13–16.

2. Linda K. Kerber, *Women of the Republic: Intellect and Ideology in Revolutionary America* (Chapel Hill, 1980), 227–31, 283–88. Although the vocabulary changed, some of the assumptions of Republican Motherhood continued into the 20th century. Sonya Michel finds that during the Depression and the Second World War, mothers were held responsible for the perpetuation of the "democratic family." Sonya Michel, "American Women and the Discourse of the Democratic Family in World War II," in Margaret Randolph Higonnet, Jane Jenson, Sonya Michel, and Margaret Collins Weitz, *Behind the Lines: Gender and the Two World Wars* (New Haven, 1987), 154–67.

3. Nancy F. Cott has explained that in antebellum America it was thought that "the success of self-government in a nation of diverse characters, dependent on majority rule, required 'the culture of the heart, the discipline of the passions, the regulation of the feelings and the affections.'" In short, political self-government required personal self-government. In fact, political self-government called for the same middle-class virtues of restraint and self-discipline that were coming to define true manhood. Cott adds that the "purpose of women's vocation was to stabilize society by generating and regenerating moral character." Nancy F. Cott, *The Bonds of*

Womanhood: "Woman's Sphere" in New England, 1780–1835 (New Haven, 1977), 96–97.

Patriots needed a mother's education in feeling more than in thought. The task facing mothers was considered so crucial to the nation that virtue itself was feminized. Lori D. Ginzberg points out that 19th century American culture "conflated ideas about femininity with ideas about morality itself." "The ideology of female moral superiority," she says, "was a central component of nineteenth-century domesticity, or the 'cult of true womanhood.'" Lori D. Ginzberg, *Women and the Work of Benevolence: Morality, Politics, and Class in the Nineteenth-Century United States* (New Haven, 1990), 1, 12. In *Frontier Women,* Julie Roy Jeffrey summarizes this way of viewing women: "As feeling, rather than thinking, creatures, lacking egotism and pride, women were uniquely able to perceive and act upon moral truth." Julie Roy Jeffrey, *Frontier Women: The Trans-Mississippi West, 1840–1880* (New York, 1979), 6.

Jeffrey's book demonstrates that domesticity was not simply the ideology of the Northeast middle class; see also Johnny Faragher and Christine Stansell, "Women and Their Families on the Overland Trail to California and Oregon, 1842–1867," *Feminist Studies,* vol. 2, no. 2/3 (1975): 150–66. Sally McMurry shows how the conditions of rural life created an ideal of "rural domesticity." Sally McMurry, *Families and Farmhouses in 19th Century America* (New York, 1988), 57. For a discussion of the place of the Bible in American ideology, including domesticity, see Judith Amanda Hunter, "Before Pluralism: The Political Culture of Nativism in Antebellum Philadelphia," dissertation, YaleUniversity, 1991, particularly pp. 215–16. Judith Hunter pointed out the centrality of common schooling to me in the history department lounge at Princeton University in March 1992; for an account of the common school reform movement, see Carl F. Kaestle, *Pillars of the Republic: Common Schools and American Society, 1780–1860* (n. p., 1983).

4. Richard Crawford, ed., *The Civil War Songbook: Complete Original Sheet Music for 37 Songs* (New York, 1977), 100–103.

5. For rural homes, see McMurry, *Families and Farmhouses.* For "Just Before the Battle Mother," see Crawford, *Civil War Songbook,* 49–52.

6. I have subtitled this book "the northern soldier leaves home," not "the Union soldier leaves home," because it is primarily a study of 19th-century northern culture. Not all Union soldiers were northerners. While white southern Union soldiers shared the political allegiance of their northern counterparts, it is not at all clear that they shared other aspects of their culture; indeed, in some ways white southern Unionism drew on those areas

of southern culture the furtherest removed from northern popular culture. It is even more unlikely that black Union soldiers, most of them southern-born, or immigrant Union soldiers came from a culture identical to that of many white northerners.

Furthermore, it should be clear that while we cannot assume that white and black southern Unionists, immigrants, and even Confederates did hold the beliefs I am calling domestic ideology, we cannot assume that they did not. I am simply drawing conclusions about the people I am studying, not about other people.

There is even a reasonable objection to the notion of "northern culture" as the North was divided by race, region, class, ethnicity, sex, and so on. Whatever the economic status of those literate northern soldiers whose letters, diaries, and memoirs I have read, most of them did share a culture that might well be called middle-class. Loosening middle-class culture from the middle class might also offend some readers. Here I am following numerous predecessors—indeed predecessors too many to number—in characterizing the 19th-century United States, if not all 19th-century Americans, as a society imbued with middle-class values. Charles Sellers has summed up the central issue neatly. "The so-called middle class was constituted not by mode and relations of production but by ideology. Where nobilities and priesthoods left folk cultures little disturbed, capital feeding on human efforts claimed hegemony over all classes. A numerous and dispersed bourgeoisie of small-scale enterprisers pushed both themselves and their workers to staggering effort by mythologizing class as a moral category. Scorning both the handful of idle rich and the multitude of dissolute poor, they apotheosized a virtuous middle class of the effortful." Sellers prefers to use "middle class" not as "a category of structure" but one of "consciousness." Charles Sellers, *The Market Revolution: Jacksonian America, 1815–1846* (New York, 1991), 237, 443.

Since literacy was prized and inculcated by the middle class, it is not surprising that literate soldiers displayed other middle-class values as well. But here it is well to note that literacy was widespread within the North—an estimated 94 percent of the population in the free states were literate—and hardly unusual among white southerners. James M. McPherson, *Ordeal by Fire: The Civil War and Reconstruction* (New York, 1982), 24. (The percentage of literacy among free southerners was 83 percent.) Most of the specific soldiers whose words you are about to read came from "middling" backgrounds. More generally, the northern soldiers whose attitudes I consider in this book were representative of the society that created them.

Chapter One

1. Mildren Throne, ed., *The Civil War Diary of Cyrus F. Boyd, Fifteenth Iowa Infantry, 1861–1863* (Millwood, N.Y., 1977), 6. For an example of two 20th-century historians interpreting a northern soldier's experience in similar ways, see Harry F. Jackson and Thomas F. O'Donnell, *Back Home in Oneida: Hermon Clarke and His Letters* (Syracuse, N.Y., 1965), vii.

2. For example, in Utica, New York in the 1850s, 40 percent of native-born males between the ages of fifteen and thirty still lived at home. Mary P. Ryan, *Cradle of the Middle Class: The Family in Oneida County, New York, 1790–1865* (New York, 1981), 167; also Tables E.4 and E.5., p. 269. What term to use to describe these older boys and young men is problematic. Joseph F. Kett uses the terms "dependence" and "semidependence," although he prefers the latter term for youth who have left home temporarily but are still bound to it; another—contemporary—term, for those males in their teens or beyond who are still at home is "large boys." Kett also reminds us that physical maturation occurred later in the antebellum period than it does now; a male in his early twenties was more likely to keep growing. Finally, the period around the Civil War saw the rise of the notion of adolescence—without, however, the use of the word "adolescence." Joseph F. Kett, *Rites of Passage: Adolescence in America 1790 to the Present* (New York, 1979).

3. Gerald F. Linderman, *Embattled Courage: The Experience of Combat in the American Civil War* (New York, 1987), 26.

4. Michael Howard, *War in European History* (Oxford, 1983), 8. Arthur H. DeRosier, Jr., *Through the South with a Union Soldier* (Johnson City, Tenn., 1969), 91. James M. McPherson, *Ordeal by Fire: The Civil War and Reconstruction* (New York, 1982), 357.

5. *Boyd Diary*, 13–21.

6. Thomas Evans Diary, February 23, 1862. Library of Congress.

7. *Boyd Diary*, 16, 123. Accounts of drunkenness and prostitution run throughout Boyd's diary.

8. William Grilfillan Gavin, *Infantryman Pettit: The Civil War Letters of Corporal Frederick Pettit* (New York, 1991), 8. *Boyd Diary*, 24–25. On middle-class youth adopting a policy of sexual restraint, see Ryan, *Cradle*, 179–80. On military vices, see William H. McNeill, *The Pursuit of Power: Technology, Armed Force, and Society Since A. D. 1000* (Chicago, 1982), 138.

9. For a discussion of the centrality of self-discipline to manliness, see E. Anthony Rotundo, "Learning About Manhood: Gender Ideals and the

Middle Class Family in Nineteenth Century America," J. A. Mangan and James Walvin, eds., *Manliness and Morality: Middle Class Masculinity in Britain and America, 1800–1940* (New York, 1987), 35–51; for its centrality to evangelical culture in the North, see Daniel Walker Howe, "The Evangelical Movement and Political Culture in the North During the Second Party System," *The Journal of American History,* March 1991, 1216–39. A more trenchant account than Howe's is Charles Sellers, *The Market Revolution: Jacksonian America, 1815–1846* (New York, 1991), 237–68. For an opposing viewpoint, David G. Pugh, *Sons of Liberty: The Masculine Mind in Nineteenth Century America* (Westport, Conn., 1983), which discusses American masculinity in terms of "the Jacksonian man." The importance of self-discipline and obedience in antebellum schooling is discussed by Carl F. Kaestle, in *Pillars of the Republic: Common Schools and American Society, 1780–1860* (n. p., 1983), 75–103. For the feminine image of the South in the postwar period, see Nina Silber, "Intemperate Men, Spiteful Women, and Jefferson Davis: Northern Views of the Defeated South," *American Quarterly* 41, No. 4 (December 1989). Anne Norton argues for a "femininized" South in *Alternative Americas: A Reading of Antebellum Political Culture* (Chicago, 1986), 132–99. The way 19th-century northern discussion of manhood could set up "Women," "Negroes," "Slaves," "Children," "Indians," "Irish," or "Southerners"—to name only a few—in opposition to "True Men" is too complicated and troublesome to deal with in this essay.

10. *Boyd Diary,* 10, 25.

11. Ibid., 23–42.

12. Ibid., 59.

13. Ibid., 123–25.

14. K. Jack Bauer, *Soldiering: The Civil War Diary of Rice C. Bull, 123rd New York Volunteer Infantry* (San Rafael, Calif., 1977), 86.

15. George C. Lawson to wife, April 29, 1864. George C. Lawson Papers in Robert Shaw Collection. Atlanta Historical Society.

16. Sidney O. Little to Sarah P. Durant, December 19, 1862. Little Letters. Schoff Collection, Clements Library, University of Michigan. Benjamen F. Ashenfelter to Father, August 23, 1863. Benjamen F. Ashenfelter Papers. Harrisburg Civil War Round Table Collection, U. S. Army Military History Institute. Marcia M. Reid-Green, ed., *Henry Matrau of the Iron Brigade* (University of Nebraska Press, forthcoming). Wilbur Fisk, *Anti-Rebel: The Civil War Letters of Wilbur Fisk* (Croton-on-Hudson, N.Y., 1983), 306. Donald J. Mrozek, "The Habit of Victory: The American Military and the Cult of Manliness," Mangan and Walvin, eds., *Manliness and Morality,* 220–39.

17. John Michael Priest, *Captain James Wren's Civil War Diary: From New Bern to Fredericksburg* (New York, 1991), 158–59.

18. Burage Rice Diary, October 9, 1861. New-York Historical Society. Bauer, *Soldiering,* ix. See George B. Forgie, *Patricide in the House Divided: A Psychological Interpretation of Lincoln and His Age* (New York, 1979), for extended discussion of the concept of the Union as a paternal legacy that in many ways burdened its heirs, the generation of 1861.

19. Henry H. Seys to Harriet Seys, October, 23, 1863. Henry H. Seys Letters. Schoff Collection, Clements Library, University of Michigan. See Ryan, *Cradle,* 155–65, for a discussion of just how much of the burden of character development middle-class thought placed on a son's mother. Also see Michael Grossberg, *Governing the Hearth: Law and the Family in Nineteenth-Century America* (Chapel Hill, 1985), for a discussion of the changing perception of the "republican family" in 19th-century America.

20. Fisk, *Anti-Rebel,* iii.

21. George W. Crosley to Edna, April 10, 1862. The Civil War Miscellany Papers. U.S. Army Military History Institute. Henry C. Metzger to sister, August 25, 1864. Henry C. Metzger Letters. Harrisburg Civil War Round Table Collection, U. S. Army Military History Institute. Margaret Brobst Roth, ed., *Well Mary: Civil War Letters of a Wisconsin Volunteer* (University of Wisconsin, Madison, 1960), 135–36. For a general discussion of northern images of the South—although one that does not use gender or familial terms—see Reid Mitchell, *Civil War Soldiers* (New York, 1988), 24–55, 90–147.

22. Mrs. C. E. McKay, *Stories of Hospital and Camp* (Freeport, N.Y., 1971; reprint of Philadelphia, 1876 ed.), viii.

23. George M. Fredrickson, *The Inner Civil War: Northern Intellectuals and the Crisis of the Union* (New York, 1965), 217–38; Leander Stillwell, *The Story of a Common Soldier of Army Life in the Civil War, 1861–1865,* 2nd ed. (n.p., 1920), 135; Linderman, *Embattled Courage,* 275–97.

Chapter Two

1. George Kies to wife, April 25, [1863], April 29, [1863], George Kies to wife, June 10, 1863. George Kies Papers. Connecticut Historical Society.

2. An outstanding overview of Union soldiers is Bell I. Wiley, *The Life of Billy Yank* (Indianapolis, 1952). Bruce Catton also helped pioneer the

study of the soldiers' perspective in his Army of the Potomac trilogy. James I. Robertson, *Soldiers Blue and Gray* (Columbia, S.C., 1988), continues working in the Bell Wiley tradition. Joseph T. Glatthaar analyzes the soldiers in Sherman's army in *The March to the Sea and Beyond: Sherman's Troops in the Savannah and Carolinas Campaigns* (New York and London, 1985). A study that focuses on the ideological motivations for the Union war effort is Earl Hess, *Liberty, Virtue, and Progress* (New York, 1988). Randall Jimerson, *The Private Civil War* (Baton Rouge, 1988) and Reid Mitchell, *Civil War Soldiers* (New York, 1988) emphasize the common attitudes and experiences of Union and Confederate soldiers. Gerald F. Linderman, *Embattled Courage* (New York, 1987) considers the experience of combat in detail.

3. A particularly good discussion of this is Eric J. Leed, *No Man's Land: Combat and Identity in World War One* (Cambridge, 1979), 1–38.

4. See Paddy Griffith's discussion of the "regimental matrix." Paddy Griffith, *Battle Tactics of the Civil War* (New Haven and London, 1989), chap. 4.

5. John R. Hunt Diary, January 22, 1862. Schoff Collection, Clements Library, University of Michigan. Ichabod Frisbie to wife, November 18, 1862. Civil War Miscellany. U.S. Army Military History Institute. (See *The Key West New Era,* April 5, 1862, in the William W. Geety Papers, Harrisburg Civil War Round Table Collection, U.S. Army Military History Institute, for notice of a debate to be held on the same subject. Diary, March 14, 21, 22, 23, 25, 25, 1862.) Richard Henry Pratt Papers. Library of Congress. Diary, April 1, 1863, April 10, 1863. Francis M. Troth Papers. University of Texas. George H. Allen Diary, October 19, 1862. University of Texas.

6. The role of officers, inspiration, and discipline in 19th-century combat is discussed in John Keegan, *The Face of Battle* (1976), chap. 3, "Infantry vs. Infantry" (pp. 162–94 in the Penguin edition).

7. Allan Nevins, ed., *A Diary of Battle: The Personal Journals of Colonel Charles S. Wainwright, 1861–1865* (New York, 1962), vii. George Anthony to Ben Anthony, October 14, 1864. George Anthony Letters. Schoff Collection, Clements Library, University of Michigan. William H. Bradbury to wife, September 13, 1862, September 26, 1862, October 10, 1862. William H. Bradbury Papers. Library of Congress.

8. John Pierson to wife, August 15, 1862. John Pierson Letters. Schoff Collection, Clements Library, University of Michigan. Albert Wilder to William and Sarah, March 26, 1863. Albert Wilder Letters. Schoff Collection, Clements Library, University of Michigan.

9. Mitchell, *Civil War Soldiers,* 11–23.

10. Silas W. Browning to wife, December 10, 1862. Silas W. Browning Papers. Library of Congress. Numa Barned to A. Barned, March 27, 1863. Numa Barned Letters. Schoff Collection, Clements Library, University of Michigan. Capt. Robert Goldthwaite Carter, *Four Soldiers in Blue: Or Sunshine and Shadows of the War of the Rebellion, a Story of the Great War from Bull Run to Appomattox* (1913; reprint Austin, 1978), 141. George C. Chandler to uncle, December 19, 1864. Civil War Miscellany. U.S. Army Military History Institute.

11. Arthur H. DeRosier, Jr., *Through the South with a Union Soldier* (Johnson City, Tenn., 1969), 40. J. P. Ray, *The Diary of a Dead Man, 1862–1864* (Eastern Acorn Press, 1976), 78. John Griffith Jones to parents, March 6, 1863. John Griffith Jones Papers. Library of Congress. Frank Badger to Sister Mary, October 28, 1862. Alfred M. Badger Papers. Library of Congress. For examples of letters and newspapers circulating throughout a company, Theodore Preston to Edward Preston, March 10, 1862. Jacob Preston Papers. Michigan Historical Collections, University of Michigan; Orra B. Bailey to wife, January 1, 1863. Orra B. Bailey Papers. Library of Congress.

12. Edward Marcus, ed., *A New Canaan Private in the Civil War: Letters of Justus M. Silliman, 17th Connecticut Volunteers* (New Canaan, Conn., 1984), 25. William Hamilton to mother, December 28, 1862. William Hamilton Papers. Library of Congress.

13. Stephen E. Ambrose, ed., *A Wisconsin Boy in Dixie: The Selected Letters of James K. Newton* (Madison, 1961), 16–20.

14. Leander Stillwell, *The Story of a Common Soldier of Army Life in the Civil War, 1861–1865*, 2nd ed., (n.p., 1920), 46.

15. Uretta A. McWhorter to William Delong, January 15, 1865, George Anthony to Ben Anthony, January 21, 1865. George Anthony Letters. Schoff Collection, Clements Library, University of Michigan. Harry F. Jackson and Thomas F. O'Donnell, *Back Home in Oneida: Hermon Clarke and His Letters* (Syracuse, N.Y., 1965), 158.

16. John E. Lowery Diary, February, March, April 1863. Harrisburg Civil War Round Table Collection. U.S. Army Military History Institute.

17. David Seibert to Pa, August 7, 1863. Seibert Family Papers. Harrisburg Civil War Round Table Collection, U.S. Army Military History Institute. DeRosier, *Through the South,* 153. John Crosby to Abby J. Crosby, February 11, 1863. John Crosby Papers. Connecticut Historical Society. Andrew Sproul to Fannie, December 3, 1862. Andrew Sproul Papers. Southern Historical Collection, University of North Carolina.

18. Stillwell, *Story of a Common Soldier,* 76. William Grilfillan Gavin,

Infantryman Pettit: The Civil War Letters of Corporal Frederick Pettit (New York, 1991), 78.

19. For a fuller discussion, see Mitchell, *Civil War Soldiers,* 56–89.

20. See Thomas R. Kemp, "Community and War: The Civil War Experience of Claremont, New Hampshire, and Newport, New Hampshire," in Maris A. Vinovskis, *Toward A Social History of the American Civil War: Exploratory Essays* (Cambridge, 1990), 31–77; Emily J. Harris, "Sons and Soldiers: Deerfield, Massachusetts, and the Civil War," *Civil War History* 30, no. 2, June 1984, pp. 157–71.

21. Henry S. Carroll to mother, March 29, 1863. Henry S. Carroll Papers. Harrisburg Civil War Round Table Collection, U.S. Army Military History Institute. H. R. Hoyt to brother, April 11, 1863. Civil War Miscellany. U. S. Army Military History Institute. Park H. Fryer to brother, March 20, 1864. Civil War Miscellany. U.S. Army Military History Institute. Diary, 1862. Andrew J. Sproul Papers. Southern Historical Collection, University of North Carolina. Wayne. C. Temple, ed., *The Civil War Letters of Henry C. Bear: A Soldier in the 116th Illinois Volunteer Infantry* (Harrogate, Tenn., 1961), 37. Lyman Foster to Mary, March 15, 1863. Civil War Miscellany. U.S. Army Military History Institute.

22. Patrick McGlenn to John Brislin, February 19, 1862. John Brislin Letters. Harrisburg Civil War Round Table Collection, U.S. Army Military History Institute.

23. Leander Chapin to Mrs. Amelia Chapin, February [probably March] 2, 1864. Albert A. Andrews Papers. Connecticut Historical Society. James R. French to parents, February 22, 1864. Albert Wilder Letters. Schoff Collection, Clements Library, University of Michigan.

24. Glatthaar, *March to the Sea,* 43. Paul Oliver to mother, November 12, 1864. Paul Ambrose Oliver Papers. Princeton University. Abram F. Conant to wife and daughter, January 9, 1863. Abram F. Conant Papers. Library of Congress.

25. Mitchell, *Civil War Soldiers,* 81.

26. Glatthaar, *March to the Sea,* 6–7, 120.

27. See Glatthaar, ibid., for a thorough discussion of the northern soldier during Sherman's march. Without using the specific idea of home, there is a lengthy discussion of the alien appearance of the southern landscape in Mitchell, *Civil War Soldiers,* chap. 4. For slavery and the family, consider Harriet Beecher Stowe's *Uncle Tom's Cabin.*

28. For a "familial" interpretation of the sectional conflict, see George B. Forgie, *Patricide in the House Divided: A Psychological Interpretation of Lincoln and His Age* (New York, 1979). For the relationship between northern small towns and American institutions, see William R. Brock, *Conflict*

and Transformation: The United States, 1844–1877 (Baltimore, 1973), 132–34.

Chapter Three

1. Mildren Throne, ed., *The Civil War Diary of Cyrus F. Boyd, Fifteenth Iowa Infantry, 1861–1863* (Millwood, N.Y., 1977).

2. Warren Wilkinson, *Mother, May You Never See the Sights I Have Seen: The Fifty-Seventh Massachusetts Veteran Volunteers in the Army of the Potomac, 1864–1865* (New York, 1990), reveals much about Irish soldiers. See Joseph T. Glatthaar, *Forged in Battle: The Civil War Alliance of Black Soldiers and White Officers* (New York, 1990), for an account of black soldiers.

3. Paul Oliver to Sam, November 10, 1862. Paul Ambrose Oliver Papers. Princeton University.

4. Levi Kent Diary, December 29, 1861; January 1, January 28, 1862. Schoff Collection, Clements Library, University of Michigan.

5. John S. Willey to wife, December 23, 1863. Norman Daniels Collection. Harrisburg Civil War Round Table Collection, U.S. Army Military History Institute.

6. David Nichol to father, September 10, 1863. David Nichol Papers. Harrisburg Civil War Round Table Collection, U.S. Army Military History Institute.

7. James W. Hildreth to mother, March 14, 1863. James W. Hildreth Papers, D. Flinbaugh Collection. Harrisburg Civil War Round Table Collection, U. S. Army Military History Institute.

8. John Crosby to Abby J. Crosby, January 17, 1863. John Crosby Papers. Connecticut Historical Society. Amos Downing to P. Downing, October 20, 1861. Civil War Miscellany. U.S. Army Military History Institute.

9. Lucien P. Waters to parents, July 13, 1862. Lucien P. Waters Papers. New-York Historical Society.

10. John Pierson to wife and daughter, September 8, 1863. John Pierson Letters. Schoff Collection, Clements Library, University of Michigan.

11. William P. Patterson to friend Thom, March 27, 1862. Civil War Miscellany. U.S. Army Military History Institute. Henry Pippitt to Rebecca Pippitt, June 20, 1864. Henry Pippitt Letters. Schoff Collection, Clements

Library, University of Michigan. Arthur H. DeRosier, Jr., *Through the South with a Union Soldier* (Johnson City, Tenn., 1969), 67–68.

12. Ashley Halsey, ed., *A Yankee Private's Civil War by Robert Hale Strong* (Chicago, 1961), 96. Harry F. Jackson and Thomas F. O'Donnell, *Back Home in Oneida: Hermon Clarke and His Letters* (Syracuse, N.Y., 1965), 39, 41.

13. Christopher Howser Keller to Caroline M. Hull, January 18, 1863. Christopher Keller Letters. Schoff Collection, Clements Library, University of Michigan.

14. Reynolds Griffin to Sister Jennie, December 13, 1862. Griffin Letters. Schoff Collection, Clements Library, University of Michigan.

15. Frederick D. Williams, *The Wild Life of the Army: Civil War Letters of James A. Garfield* (East Lansing, 1964), 87.

16. Ibid., 42, 69.

17. Leander Stillwell, *The Story of a Common Soldier of Army Life in the Civil War, 1861–1865,* 2nd ed. (n.p., 1920), 262–63. Henry H. Eby, *Observations of an Illinois Boy in Battle, Camp, and Prisons—1861 to 1865* (n.p., 1910), 36.

18. Twentieth Massachusetts Volunteers, Tribute to Col. Revere on his death (1863), P. J. Revere Papers. Massachusetts Historical Society.

Chapter Four

1. Thomas Wentworth Higginson, *Army Life in a Black Regiment* (orig. published 1869; reprint ed., New York, 1984), 53, 244.

2. This biographical sketch is drawn from Howard N. Meyer's introduction to Higginson, *Army Life,* 9–25; the Higginson quotation is on page 29.

3. Higginson, *Army Life,* 33, 35, 73–74, 78–79. Other white men preferred racially mixed soldiers. "If you should ask me for the type of an admirable soldier, I would present you with the Mulatto. It seems that he unites in himself, physically speaking, the perfection of both races." "Notes on Colored Troops and Military Colonies on Southern Soil by an Officer of the 9th Army Corps" (New York, 1863).

4. Higginson, *Army Life,* 35–36, 51, 128, 134.

5. Ibid., 30, 41, 51. Others went farther than Higginson in their advocacy of southern black soldiers over northern. Bostonian Samuel Storrow regretted that the 54th Massachusetts Volunteers recruited any Massa-

chusetts black men. Northern black men were, he said, "in comparison with their southern brethren, utterly deficient in those qualities of body and constitution which it was supposed would fit them for a military life"—i.e. acclimation to the South and an aptitude for "rigorous discipline and blind obedience." Massachusetts black men, not trained to slavery, were "enervated and licentious, and undesirable for soldiers." This judgment may be one reason Storrow did not apply for a commission in the 54th. Samuel Storrow to parents, March 27, 1863. Samuel Storrow Papers, Massachusetts Historical Society.

6. Higginson, *Army Life,* 72, 246.

7. Ibid., 70–71.

8. Ibid., 160. For a discussion of true manhood, see chap. 1. For a discussion of the attitudes of white abolitionists toward race, see Ronald G. Walters, *The Antislavery Appeal: American Abolitionism after 1830* (New York, 1984), 54–69.

9. Higginson, *Army Life,* 53.

10. Ibid., 69–70.

11. Ibid., 236.

12. Ibid., 54

13. Ibid., 123–24.

14. Ibid., 251.

15. Ibid., 74, 232, 249.

16. Ibid., 233–235.

17. Meyer's introduction to Higginson, *Army Life,* 18, 21–22.

18. Ira Berlin, Joseph P. Reidy, and Leslie S. Rowland, eds., *Freedom: A Documentary History of Emancipation, 1861–1867,* Series II: The Black Military Experience (Cambridge, 1982), 412–14, 417–18, 420–21. Luis F. Emilio, *A Brave Black Regiment: History of the Fifty-Fourth Massachusetts Volunteer Infantry, 1863–1865* (New York, 1992), 23, 335. See Joseph T. Glatthaar, *Forged in Battle: The Civil War Alliance of Black Soldiers and White Officers* (New York, 1990), 81–84, for additional discussion of racism among the white officers.

19. Berlin, Reidy, and Rowland, *Freedom,* 22; for additional discussion of the relationship between white officers and black soldiers, see pp. 406–11; for the December 12, 1863, riot, see pp. 442–49. For another account of mutinies among black troops, see Glatthaar, *Forged in Battle,* 115–17.

20. Higginson, *Army Life,* 267–76. For an account of Walker's mutiny, see Howard C. Westwood, *Black Troops, White Commanders, and Freedmen During the Civil War* (Carbondale, Ill., 1992), 125–41; for a pay mutiny in a Rhode Island regiment, see pp. 142–66. For an example of

American soldiers from a very different culture—18th-century New Englanders—who viewed their military service in terms of contract, see Fred Anderson, *A People's Army: Massachusetts Soldiers and Society in the Seven Years' War* (Chapel Hill, 1984), 185–95.

21. Mrs. C. E. McKay, *Stories of Hospital and Camp* (Freeport, N.Y., 1971—reprint of Philadelphia, 1876 ed.), 167. Higginson, *Army Life,* 34.

22. Edmund Wilson, *Patriotic Gore: Studies in the Literature of the American Civil War* (London, 1987; orig. pub. 1962), 615.

Chapter Five

1. John S. Willey to wife, March 20, 1864. Norman Daniels Collection, Harrisburg Civil War Round Table Collection, U.S. Army Military History Institute. Oscar Cram to Ellen, April 3, 1864. Civil War Miscellany, U.S. Army Military History Institute.

2. Caleb Blanchard to wife, September 8, 1862. Caleb Blanchard Papers. Connecticut Historical Society.

3. Lyman C. Holford Diary, July 31, 1862. Library of Congress. S. H. Eels to uncle and aunt, April 28, 1861. S. H. Eels Papers. Library of Congress. [Theophilus Parsons], *Memoirs of Emily Elizabeth Parsons* (Boston, 1880), 62–63. John William De Forest, *Miss Ravenel's Conversion from Secession to Loyalty,* edited by Gordon S. Haight (New York, 1955), 326–27. Lieut.-Colonel F. F. Cavada, *Libby Life: Experiences of a Prisoner of War in Richmond, Va., 1863–1864* (reprint of 1865 ed.; Lanham, Md., 1985), 44–46. John Wesley Marshall Journal. September 13, 1863. Library of Congress.

4. Orra B. Bailey to wife, January 1, 1863. Orra B. Bailey Papers. Library of Congress. Allen Woods Miller Diary, January 4, 1863. Library of Congress. Wilbur Fisk, "Oration—Decoration Day, Alden, Minnesota, May 31, 1891," copy in author's possession.

5. The literature on domesticity is extensive. See Nancy F. Cott, *The Bonds of Womanhood: "Woman's Sphere" in New England, 1780–1835* (New Haven, 1977), 63–100. For additional discussion of 19th-century notions of child rearing, see Barbara Leslie Epstein, *The Politics of Domesticity: Women, Evangelism, and Temperance in Nineteenth Century America* (Middletown, Conn., 1981), 67–87.

6. Two articles are essential: One is in John R. Brumgardt, ed., *Civil War Nurse: The Diary and Letters of Hannah Ropes* (Knoxville, 1980).

Brumgardt's opening essay is both an excellent introduction to Civil War nursing and a sensitive account of the way nursing brought women into the masculine sphere. The other is Ann Douglas Wood, "The War Within a War: Women Nurses in the Union Army," *Civil War History* 18, no. 3 (September 1972): pp. 197–212. Wood discusses the way that wartime nursing prompted women to challenge assumptions of masculine authority.

7. Mary A. Livermore, *My Story of the War: A Woman's Narrative of Four Years Personal Experience* (Hartford, Conn., 1890), 345–46. Mrs. C. E. McKay, *Stories of Hospital and Camp* (Freeport, N.Y., 1971; reprint of 1876 ed.), 96.

8. Louisa May Alcott, "Hospital Sketches," *Alternative Alcott* (New Brunswick, N.J., 1988), 42. *Memoirs of E. E. Parsons,* 20, 26, 89. Lori D. Ginzberg, *Women and the Work of Benevolence: Morality, Politics, and Class in the Nineteenth-Century United States* (New Haven, 1990), 144.

9. Julia S. Wheelock, *The Boys in White; The Experience of a Hospital Agent in and around Washington* (New York, 1870), 196.

10. Brumgardt, ed., *Ropes,* 61. *Memoirs of E. E. Parsons,* 88.

11. *Memoirs of E. E. Parsons,* 79. Livermore, *My Story of the War,* 169, 202. McKay, *Stories of Hospital and Camp,* 35–36. Brumgardt, ed., *Ropes,* 67–68.

12. Adelaide W. Smith, *Reminiscences of an Army Nurse During the Civil War* (New York, 1911), 85. Katharine Prescott Wormeley, *The Other Side of War with the Army of the Potomac: Letters from the Headquarters of the United States Sanitary Commission During the Peninsula Campaign in Virginia in 1862* (Boston, 1889), 118. Brumgardt, ed., *Ropes,* 53. Sister Mary Denis Maher, *To Bind Up the Wounds: Catholic Sister Nurses in the U.S. Civil War* (Westport, Conn., 1989), 139. I think that this soldier was Union, but I am not positive.

13. Brumgardt, ed., *Ropes,* 61.

14. McKay, *Stories of Hospital and Camp,* 53–54.

15. Brumgardt, ed., *Ropes,* 76, 89.

16. *Memoirs of E. E. Parsons,* 51. Wheelock, *Boys in White,* vi.

17. Phillip Shaw Paludan, *"A People's Contest": The Union and the Civil War, 1861–1865* (New York, 1988), 355.

18. K. Jack Bauer, *Soldiering: The Civil War Diary of Rice C. Bull, 123rd New York Volunteer Infantry* (San Rafael, Calif., 1977), 22–25.

19. Mildren Throne, ed., *The Civil War Diary of Cyrus F. Boyd, Fifteenth Iowa Infantry, 1861–1863* (Millwood, N.Y., 1977), 121. Arthur H. DeRosier, Jr., *Through the South with a Union Soldier* (Johnson City, Tenn., 1969), 160. Lawrence Van Alstyne, *Diary of an Enlisted Man* (New Haven, 1910), 149. Daniel Faust to sister, [between October 7 and November 7]

1862. Daniel Faust Letters. Harrisburg Civil War Round Table Collection, U.S. Army Military History Institute.

20. Horace Snow to parents, August 3, 1862. Snow Family Papers. Duke University. John Michael Priest, ed., *Captain James Wren's Civil War Diary: From New Bern to Fredericksburg* (New York, 1991), 85.

21. Alcott, *Alternative Alcott,* 39. Ann Douglas, *The Feminization of American Culture* (New York, 1977), 244.

22. William Grilfillan Gavin, *Infantryman Pettit: The Civil War Letters of Corporal Frederick Pettit* (New York, 1991), 153–55.

23. T. Harry Williams, *Selected Writings and Speeches of Abraham Lincoln* (New York, 1980), 249–50.

Chapter Six

1. Charles Royster, *The Destructive War: William Tecumseh Sherman, Stonewall Jackson, and the Americans* (New York, 1991), 20, 22.

2. Luther C. Furst Diary, April 29–May 18, 1863. Harrisburg Civil War Round Table Collection, U.S. Army Military History Institute. Albert C. Cleavland to Christopher H. Keller, August 3, 1863. Christopher H. Keller Letters. Schoff Collection, Clements Library, University of Michigan. James Boyd Jones, Jr., "A Tale of Two Cities: The Hidden Battle Against Venereal Disease in Civil War Nashville and Memphis," *Civil War History* 31, No. 3 (September 1985), pp. 270–76. George Henry Bates to William Bates, April 27, 1863. George Henry Bates Letters. Schoff Collection, Clements Library, University of Michigan.

3. Alonzo J. Sawyer Diary, January 16, 1864. Civil War Miscellany, U.S. Army Military History Institute.

4. Michael Grossberg, *Governing the Hearth: Law and the Family in Nineteenth-Century America* (Chapel Hill, 1985), 10.

5. Quoted in Barbara Leslie Epstein, *The Politics of Domesticity: Women, Evangelism, and Temperance in Nineteenth Century America* (Middletown, Conn., 1981), 85.

6. Ronald G. Walters, *The Antislavery Appeal: American Abolitionism After 1830* (New York, 1984), 71–110, discusses abolitionist attitudes toward sexuality, women, and the family in the North and South.

7. Ibid., 108–9.

8. "A Few Words in Behalf of the Loyal Women of the United States by One of Themselves" (Loyal Publication Society, No. 10, New York,

182   NOTES

1863, in Frank Freidel, *Union Pamphlets of the Civil War, 1861–1865* (Cambridge, Mass., 1967), II, 766–86. For additional discussion of northern attitudes toward secesh women, see Royster, *The Destructive War,* 86–87, and Nina Silber, "Intemperate Men, Spiteful Women, and Jefferson Davis: Northern Views of the Defeated South," *American Quarterly* 41, No. 4 (Dec. 1989).

9. Bernhard Domschcke, *Twenty Months in Captivity: Memoirs of a Union Officer in Confederate Prisons* (Rutherford, Madison, and Teaneck, N.J., 1987), 33. Leander Stillwell, *The Story of a Common Soldier of Army Life in the Civil War, 1861–1865,* 2nd ed. (n.p., 1920), 84. For a valuable discussion of attitudes toward women during the war, see Michael Fellman, *Inside War: The Guerrilla Conflict in Missouri During the American Civil War* (New York, 1989), 193–230, and "At the Nihilist Edge: Reflection on Guerrilla Warfare During the America Civil War," paper given at conference "On the Road to Total War: The American Civil War and the German Wars of Unification," German Historical Institute, Washington, D.C., April 1–4, 1992. Klaus Theweleit discusses women-hating at great length in his study of the Freikorps. Klaus Theweleit, *Male Fantasies: Volume 1: Women, Floods, Bodies, History,* translated by Stephen Conway in collaboration with Erica Carter and Chris Turner (Minneapolis, 1987), 3–204. For example, the men whom he terms "soldier males" did attribute male participation in the Red revolts to female instigation. While Theweleit's book is provocative as an analysis of fascist culture and its origins, it does not seem to me directly relevant to a study of 19th-century northern culture; nonetheless, some of his "deductions" may offer insight, such as this one exploring the psychology the soldier male who attacks a woman: *terror against a woman who is not identified with the mother/sister image is essentially self-defense* (p. 183).

10. Arthur H. DeRosier, Jr., *Through the South with a Union Soldier* (Johnson City, Tenn., 1969), 69. Paul Fatout, ed., *Letters of a Civil War Surgeon* (Purdue Universities, 1961), 38.

11. James T. Miller to Robert E. Miller, April 2, 1862. Miller Brothers Letters. Schoff Collection, Clements Library, University of Michigan.

12. The Civil War Journal of Henry F. Lewis, transcribed by Professor Richard D. Challener, Princeton University. Mildren Throne, ed., *The Civil War Diary of Cyrus F. Boyd, Fifteenth Iowa Infantry, 1861–1863* (Millwood, N.Y., 1977), 97. Rufus Mead, Jr., to friends, May 28, 1862. Rufus Mead, Jr., Papers. Library of Congress. Maurus Oestreich Diary, July 25, 1863. Harrisburg Civil War Round Table Collection, U.S. Army Military History Institute. Edward Marcus, ed., *A New Canaan Private in the Civil War:*

Letters of Justus M. Silliman, 17th Connecticut Volunteers (New Canaan, Conn., 1984), 14–15.

13. James T. Miller to Robert E. Miller, [1863–letter 8:75] Miller Brothers Letters. Schoff Collection, Clements Library, University of Michigan. Rufus Mead, Jr., to friends, December 28, 1864. Rufus Mead, Jr., Papers. Library of Congress.

14. Ashley Halsey, ed., *A Yankee Private's Civil War by Robert Hale Strong* (Chicago, 1961), 45.

15. U.S. War Department, *The War of the Rebellion: A Compilation of the Official Records of the Union and Confederate Armies,* Series II, Volume 4, p. 885.

16. Ibid., pp. 876–77, 915.

17. Worthington Chauncey Ford, ed., *War Letters, 1862–1865, of John Chipman Gray and John Codman Ropes* (Boston, 1927), 35.

18. Susan Brownmiller, *Against Our Will: Men, Women, and Rape* (1975; page reference to Bantam edition, 1990), 89.

19. Isaac Comstock Hadden to friend, April 27, 1864. Isaac Comstock Hadden Papers. New-York Historical Society. F. N. Boney, ed., *A Union Soldier in the Land of the Vanquished: The Diary of Sergeant Mathew Woodruff, June-December, 1865* (University, Ala., 1969), 19–20.

20. Fellman, *Inside War,* 199–214.

21. David C. Edmonds, ed., *The Conduct of Federal Troops in Louisiana During the Invasions of 1863 and 1864: Official Report Compiled from Sworn Testimony under Direction of Governor Henry W. Allen, Shreveport, April, 1865* (Lafayette, La., 1988), 29–30.

22. Royster also notes the rape of black women during the March to the Sea. Royster, *The Destructive War,* 23, 342.

23. Edmonds, *Conduct of Federal Troops,* 197.

24. Brownmiller, *Against Our Will,* 30–33.

25. Walters, *The Antislavery Appeal,* 71–110.

26. Joseph T. Glatthaar, *Forged in Battle: The Civil War Alliance of Black Soldiers and White Officers* (New York, 1990), 92–93, 118. Ira Berlin, Joseph P. Reidy, and Leslie S. Rowland, eds., *Freedom: A Documentary History of Emancipation, 1861–1867,* Series II: The Black Military Experience (Cambridge, 1982), 34, 767–69, 807. Brownmiller, *Against Our Will,* 133–40.

27. Edmonds, *Conduct of Federal Troops,* 61–62.

28. Ambrose Bierce, *In the Midst of Life: Tales of Soldiers and Civilians* (New York, 1927), 93–104.

29. Sandra M. Gilbert, "Soldier's Heart: Literary Men, Literary Women, and the Great War," in Margaret Randolph Higonnet, Jane Jen-

son, Sonya Michel, and Margaret Collins Weitz, *Behind the Lines: Gender and the Two World Wars* (New Haven, 1987), 197–226. For a similar discussion of the Second World War II, see Susan Gubar, "'This is My Rifle, This is My Gun': World War II and the Blitz on Women,"also in Higonnet, Jenson, Michel, and Weitz, pp. 227–59. John William De Forest, *Miss Ravenel's Conversion from Secession to Loyalty,* ed. by Gordon S. Haight (New York, 1955), 43. "A Few Words," Freidel, *Union Pamphlets,* II, 786. "The Great Union Meeting. Held at Indianapolis, February 26, 1863. Speeches of Andrew Johnson, of Tennessee, Gen. Samuel F. Carney of Ohio, and Others," in Freidel, *Union Pamphlets,* II, 565–606, quotation on p. 583. Johnson also said that southern women "had unsexed themselves and exerted more influence for the rebellion than the men."

30. Margaret Brobst Roth, ed., *Well Mary: Civil War Letters of a Wisconsin Volunteer* (University of Wisconsin, Madison, 1960), 71–72.

Chapter Seven

1. Leander Stillwell, *The Story of a Common Soldier of Army Life in the Civil War, 1861–1865,* 2nd ed., (n.p., 1920), 185–89.

2. [Ezra Mundy Hunt], "About the War. Plain Words to Plain People by a Plain Man," in Frank Freidel, *Union Pamphlets of the Civil War, 1861–1865* (Cambridge, Mass., 1967), I, 551–64; quote on p. 560. Howard Cecil Perkins, *Northern Editorials on Secession* (New York, 1942), II, 739.

3. Mary P. Ryan, *The Empire of the Mother: American Writing About Domesticity, 1830–1860* (New York, 1982), 54. Mary P. Ryan, *Cradle of the Middle Class: The Family in Oneida County, New York, 1790–1865* (New York, 1981), 159.

4. *Narrative of Privations and Sufferings of United States Officers and Soldiers while Prisoners of War in the Hands of the Rebel Authorities. Being the Report of a Commission of Inquiry Appointed by the United States Sanitary Commission* (Philadelphia, 1864), 96.

5. Felix Brannigan to sister, May 30, 1862. Felix Brannigan Papers. Library of Congress.

6. James I. Robertson, Jr., *The Civil War Letters of General Robert McAllister* (New Brunswick, N.J., 1965), 159–60, 204.

7. Albinus R. Fell to wife, April 19, 1862. Civil War Miscellany. U.S. Army Military History Institute.

8. John S. Copley to Robert Moody, July 8, 1862. John S. Copley Papers. Princeton University. Burage Rice Diary, October 9, 1861. New-York Historical Society.

9. Edward Marcus, ed., *A New Canaan Private in the Civil War: Letters of Justus M. Silliman, 17th Connecticut Volunteers* (New Canaan, Conn., 1984), 100.

10. George M. Fredrickson, *The Inner Civil War: Northern Intellectuals and the Crisis of the Union* (New York, 1965). Lori D. Ginzberg, *Women and the Work of Benevolence: Morality, Politics, and Class in the Nineteenth-Century United States* (New Haven, 1990), 133–73.

11. Harry F. Jackson and Thomas F. O'Donnell, *Back Home in Oneida: Hermon Clarke and His Letters* (Syracuse, N.Y., 1965), 176.

12. Ibid., 115–17.

13. "The Great Union Meeting. Held at Indianapolis, February 26, 1863. Speeches of Andrew Johnson, of Tennessee, Gen. Samuel F. Carney of Ohio, and Others," in Freidel, *Union Pamphlets,* II, 565–606, quotation on p. 583.

14. Frederick D. Williams, *The Wild Life of the Army: Civil War Letters of James A. Garfield* (East Lansing, 1964), 14, 20–21. John Lothrop Motley, "The Causes of the American Civil War," in Freidel, *Union Pamphlets,* I, 29–54. Frederickson, *The Inner Civil War,* 76, 135.

15. Burage Rice Diary, January 1, 1863. New-York Historical Society. David Nichol to father and home, January 4, 1863. David Nichol Papers. Harrisburg Civil War Round Table Collection, U.S. Army Military History Institute.

16. Paul Oliver to Dudley Field, July 17, 1862. Paul Ambrose Oliver Papers. Princeton University.

17. Joseph Orville Jackson, ed., *"Some of the Boys . . . :" The Civil War Letters of Isaac Jackson, 1862–1865* (Carbondale, Ill., 1960), 133.

18. John William De Forest, *Miss Ravenel's Conversion from Secession to Loyalty,* edited by Gordon S. Haight (New York, 1955), 10.

19. Ibid., 84.

20. Ibid., 159.

21. Ibid., 372.

22. Ibid., 156.

23. Ibid., 397–98.

24. Ibid., 80.

25. For additional discussion of the postwar era, see Edmund Wilson, *Patriotic Gore: Studies in the Literature of the American Civil War* (London, 1987; orig. pub. 1962); Gaines Foster, *Ghosts of the Confederacy* (New York, 1987); and Nina Silber, "Intemperate Men, Spiteful Women, and

Jefferson Davis: Northern Views of the Defeated South," *American Quarterly* 41, No. 4 (December 1989).

26. E. N. Gilpin Diary, April 14, 1865. Library of Congress. S. H. Eels to uncle and aunt, April 28, 1862, S. H. Eels to Aunt Sarah, May 10, 1863. S. H. Eels Papers. Library of Congress. Rudolphe Rey to Miss Lizze De-Voe, June 3, 1865. Rudolphe Rey Papers. New-York Historical Society. See also Margaret Brobst Roth, ed., *Well Mary: Civil War Letters of a Wisconsin Volunteer* (University of Wisconsin, Madison, 1960), 84–85.

27. Frank Roberts to friend, June 8, 1863. Harrisburg Civil War Round Table Collection. U.S. Army Military History Institute. William M. Cash and Lucy Somerville Howorth, eds., *My Dear Nellie: The Civil War Letters of William L. Nugent to Eleanor Smith Nugent* (Jackson, Miss., 1977), 164–65.

28. Anne Norton discusses "familial metaphors for sectional conflict." *Alternative Americas: A Reading of Antebellum Political Culture* (Chicago, 1986), 266–73.

29. Perkins, *Northern Editorials,* II, 741.

Chapter Eight

1. Arthur H. DeRosier, Jr., ed., *Through the South with a Union Soldier* (Johnson City, Tenn., 1969), 16, 48–49, 56, 60, 64, 76, 82, 88–89, 95, 115, 126–28, 134, 140, 157–58. For Jones, see Paul Fussell, *The Great War and Modern Memory* (New York, 1975), 144–54.

2. DeRosier, *Through the South,* 51–55. For mid 19th-century burials and cemeteries, see Lawrence Taylor, "Symbolic Death: An Anthropological View of Mourning Ritual," and Donald E. Simon, "The Worldly Side of Paradise: Green-Wood Cemetery," both in Marsha V. Pike and Janice Gray Armstrong, eds., *A Time to Mourn: Expressions of Grief in Nineteenth Century America* (Stony Brook, N.Y.: The Museum at Stony Brook, 1980), 39–66.

3. James M. McPherson, *Ordeal by Fire: The Civil War and Reconstruction* (New York, 1982), 181, 488.

4. Benjamen F. Ashenfelter to mother, May 10, 1863. Benjamen F. Ashenfelter Papers. Harrisburg Civil War Round Table Collection, U. S. Army Military History Institute. William Grilfillan Gavin, *Infantryman Pettit: The Civil War Letters of Corporal Frederick Pettit* (New York, 1991), 8, 59.

5. Rufus Mead, Jr., to friends, July 23, 1861. Rufus Mead, Jr., Papers. Library of Congress. Albinus R. Fell to wife, April 19, 1862. Civil War Miscellany. U.S. Army Military History Institute. Mildren Throne, ed., *The Civil War Diary of Cyrus F. Boyd, Fifteenth Iowa Infantry, 1861–1863* (Millwood, N.Y., 1977), 67. Reuben Smith Goodman Diary, April 18, 1864. Schoff Collection, Clements Library, University of Michigan.

6. Lewis O. Saum, *The Popular Mood of Pre-Civil War America* (Westport, Conn., 1980), xxii, 3. K. Jack Bauer, *Soldiering: The Civil War Diary of Rice C. Bull, 123rd New York Volunteer Infantry* (San Rafael, Calif., 1977), 47.

7. Martha V. Pike and Janice Gray Armstrong, eds., *A Time to Mourn,* 13. DeRosier, *Through the South,* 134.

8. [Theophilus Parsons], *Memoirs of Emily Elizabeth Parsons* (Boston, 1880), 57. Phillip Shaw Paludan, *"A People's Contest": The Union and the Civil War, 1861–1865* (New York, 1988), 363–74. Jonathan LaBrant Diary, June 19–21, 1863. Civil War Miscellany, U. S. Army Military History Institute. For additional discussion of 19th century attitudes toward death, see James J. Farrell, *Inventing the American Way of Death, 1830–1920* (Philadelphia, 1980), and Ann Douglas, *The Feminization of American Culture* (New York, 1977).

9. Daniel Faust to mother, December 26, 1862. Daniel Faust Letters. Harrisburg Civil War Round Table Collection, U.S. Army Military History Institute. Richard Crawford, ed., *The Civil War Songbook: Complete Original Sheet Music for 37 Songs* (New York, 1977), 78–81. Thomas Wentworth Higginson, *Army Life in a Black Regiment* (orig. published 1869; reprint ed., New York, 1984), 45.

10. Saum, *The Popular Mood,* 92–104.

11. John William De Forest, *Miss Ravenel's Conversion from Secession to Loyalty,* edited by Gordon S. Haight (New York, 1955), 274. Reuben Smith Goodman Diary, August 22, 1864. Schoff Collection, Clements Library, University of Michigan.

12. George W. Crosley to Edna, April 10, 1862. Civil War Miscellany. U.S. Army Military History Institute.

13. Samuel Storrow to parents, January 22, 1863. Samuel Storrow Papers. Massachusetts Historical Society.

14. Pike and Armstrong, eds., *A Time to Mourn,* 11. Crawford, *Civil War Songbook,* 96–99.

15. J. P. Ray, *The Diary of a Dead Man, 1862–1864* (Eastern Acorn Press, 1976), 167–68. Lavalette Griffin to sister, May 21, 1862. Griffin Letters. Schoff Collection, Clements Library, University of Michigan.

Lawrence Van Alstyne, *Diary of an Enlisted Man* (New Haven, Conn., 1910), 32.

16. John R. Brumgardt, ed., *Civil War Nurse: The Diary and Letters of Hannah Ropes* (Knoxville, 1980), 95.

17. For another discussion of the Battle Hymn and the need to see soldiers as angels, see Paludan, "*A People's Contest*," 350–51.

18. Katharine Prescott Wormeley, *The Other Side of War with the Army of the Potomac: Letters from the Headquarters of the United States Sanitary Commission During the Peninsula Campaign inVirginia in 1862* (Boston, 1889), 72. Julia S. Wheelock, *The Boys in White; The Experience of a Hospital Agent in and around Washington* (New York, 1870), 23–25.

19. Sylia G. L. Dannett, ed., *Noble Women of the North* (New York, 1959), 302.

20. Henry Grimes Marshall to Hattie, September 11, 1864; October 9, 1865. Marshall Letters. Schoff Collection, Clements Library, University of Michigan.

21. Mrs. C. E. McKay, *Stories of Hospital and Camp* (Freeport, N.Y., 1971; reprint of Philadelphia, 1876 ed.), vii–ix, 16.

22. Brumgardt, *Civil War Nurse*, 101–2.

23. John J. Ryder, *Reminiscences of Three Years' Service in the Civil War: By a Cape Cod Boy* (New Bedford, Mass., 1928), 48.

Afterword

1. Wilbur Fisk, *Anti-Rebel: The Civil War Letters of Wilbur Fisk* (Croton-on-Hudson, 1983), 19.

2. Ibid., 207.

3. For my analysis of what are traditionally considered "military" aspects of the war—although any military consideration of the Civil War rapidly becomes technological, political, economic, and social—and specifically of the question of why the Union won, I have been strongly influenced by David Donald, ed., *Why the North Won the Civil War* (Baton Rouge, 1960), particularly Richard N. Current's "God and the Strongest Battalions"; James M. McPherson, *Ordeal by Fire: The Civil War and Reconstruction* (New York, 1982); James M. McPherson, *The Battle Cry of Freedom: The Civil War Era* (New York, 1988), and Richard E. Beringer, et al., *Why the South Lost the Civil War* (Athens, Ga., 1986); and especially, Russell Weigley, *The American Way of War: A History of United States Military*

Strategy and Policy (New York, 1973). While not about the Civil War, John Keegan, *The Face of Battle* (New York, 1976), is indispensable for understanding how armies work. Phillip Shaw Paludan, *"A People's Contest": The Union and the Civil War, 1864–1865* (New York, 1988), is crucial for understanding the Union war effort. Much of my thinking about the Confederacy comes from pushing against Emory M. Thomas's intelligent and provocative interpretation; see his *The Confederate Nation 1861–1865* (New York, 1979). If there is one historian I am self-consciously following in my understanding of the Confederacy at war, it is Bell Irvin Wiley, particularly his *Plain People of the Confederacy* (Gloucester, Mass., 1971), but also *The Road to Appomattox* (New York, 1986), *Southern Negroes 1861–1865* (New Haven, 1938), and *The Life of Johnny Reb* (Indianapolis, 1943). I have learned much from his *Life of Billy Yank* (Indianapolis, 1952), and from newer work on the soldiers of the Civil War—Earl Hess, *Liberty, Virtue, and Progress* (New York, 1988), Randall Jimerson, *The Private Civil War* (Baton Rouge, 1988), and Gerald Linderman, *Embattled Courage* (New York, 1987). Finally, I learned a lot writing *Civil War Soldiers* (New York, 1988).

4. My thinking here has been influenced by Phillip Shaw Paludan, *"A People's Contest,"* particularly chapter one, "Communities Go to War." He makes the point about the postmaster on p. 12.

5. Ibid., 15–18; McPherson, *Battle Cry of Freedom,* 286.

6. Fisk, *Anti-Rebel,* 7.

7. Weigley, *The American Way of War,* 139.

8. McPherson, *Ordeal by Fire,* 411. Grant remembered Lincoln's phrase as "As we say out West, if a man can't skin he must hold a leg while somebody else does." E. B. Long, ed., *Personal Memoirs of U. S. Grant* (New York: Da Capo Press, 1982), 373.

9. Fisk, *Anti-Rebel,* 87.

10. Those wishing to understand the human cost of the latter third of the war might well begin with Warren Wilkinson's splendid *Mother, May You Never See the Sights I Have Seen: The Fifty-Seventh Massachusetts Veteran Volunteers in the Army of the Potomac, 1864–1865* (New York, 1990).

11. Lawrence Van Alstyne, *Diary of an Enlisted Man* (New Haven, 1910), 41.

12. The phrase "founding a nation in blood" comes from Charles Royster, "Founding a Nation in Blood: Military Conflict and American Nationality," in Ronald Hoffman and Peter Albert, eds., *Arms and Independence: The Military Character of the American Revolution* (Charlottesville, 1984)—which is also a discussion of the First Inaugural. T. Harry Williams, *Selected Writings and Speeches of Abraham Lincoln* (New York, 1980), 114–24.

13. William Gilfillan Gavin, *Infantryman Pettit: The Civil War Letters of Corporal Frederick Pettit* (New York, 1991), 123.

14. Even operations like Sherman's March to the Sea or the campaign of the Carolinas demanded an ideological commitment on the part of the soldiers. Armies like Sherman's relied on foraging to feed themselves. Old Regime commanders usually did not dare supply their armies by foraging, because the soldiers were too unlikely to come back to face battle and military discipline. See William H. McNeill, *The Pursuit of Power: Technology, Armed Force, and Society Since A. D. 1000* (Chicago, 1982), 159–60.

15. Clifford Dowdey and Louis H. Manarin, eds., *The Wartime Papers of R. E. Lee* (Boston, 1961), 938–39. Charles Fenton James to Emma, February 7, 1865. Charles Fenton James Papers. Southern Historical Collection, University of North Carolina.

16. John R. Marley to father, April 13, 1863. Confederate States of America Archives: Army-Miscellany: Officers and Soldiers Letters. Duke University. G. W. Philips to mother and sister, June 19, 1864. Confederate States of America Archives: Army-Miscellany: Officers and Soldiers Letters. Duke University. Neill McLeod to brother, July 19, 1863. Neill McLeod Papers. Southern Historical Collection, University of North Carolina.

17. Drew Gilpin Faust, "Altars of Sacrifice: Confederate Women and the Narrative of War," *Journal of American History* 76, No. 4 (March 1990): 1200–1228. Buck Long to Sawney Webb, August 10, 1863. Webb Family Papers. Southern Historical Collection, University of North Carolina. Charles Fenton James to Emma, February 13, 1865. Charles Fenton James Papers. Southern Historical Collection, University of North Carolina. John Paris, *A Sermon Preached Before Brig-Gen. Hoke's Brigade at Kinston, N.C., on the 28th of February, 1864 . . . Upon the Death of Twenty-Two Men Who Had Been Executed in the Presence of the Brigade for the Crime of Desertion* (Greensborough, N.C., 1864). Copy in John Paris Papers. Southern Historical Collection, University of North Carolina. Taylor quoted in Alan T. Nolan, *Lee Considered: General Robert E. Lee and Civil War History* (Chapel Hill, 1991), 45. See also Donna Rebecca Dondes Krug, *The Folks Back Home: The Confederate Homefront During the Civil War* (Columbia, S.C., forthcoming).

18. Bell Irvin Wiley, ed., *"This Infernal War": The Confederate Letters of Sgt. Edwin H. Fay* (Austin, 1958), 96, 292, 302.

19. William M. Cash and Lucy Somerville Howarth, eds., *My Dear Nellie: The Civil War Letters of William L. Nugent to Eleanor Smith Nugent* (Jackson, Miss., 1977), 117–18, 136.

20. John A. Cato to wife, March 11, 1863. The Civil War Miscellany Papers. U.S. Army Military History Institute. Bell Irvin Wiley discusses

violence of blacks against whites in areas reached by the Union army in *The Plain People of the Confederacy,* 74–82; Clarence L. Mohr discusses rumors of insurrection, black violence, and the trouble women had as slave managers in *On the Threshold of Freedom: Masters and Slaves in Civil War Georgia* (Athens, Ga., 1986), 214–32.

21. T. Harry Williams, *Selected Writings and Speeches of Abraham Lincoln* (New York, 1980), 250–56. For additional discussion of Lee's delay in surrendering and the price the South paid for it, see Nolan, *Lee Considered,* 112–33.

Index

193

Blacks (*Cont.*)

  emotionalism of, 59–60; equality of, 62–63, 67; and the familial metaphor, 133; and fatherhood, 64; feminine virtues in black men, 59; and manhood, 59–60, 63–64; northern vs. southern, 58; and officer–soldier relations, 43, 57–69; and paternalism, 57–69; as property, 108; rape of, 104, 106–9, 110; as rapists, 109–10; rebellion/riots by, 66–67, 164–65; religion of, 58, 59; skin color of, 56–57, 63; in the Union army, 42, 56–70; views of soldiering by, 66–67

Boyd, Cyrus F., 3, 17, 39–42, 82, 90, 99, 139

Boyd, Scott, 9

The Boys in White: The Experience of a Hospital Agent in and around Washington (Wheelock), 148

Brannigan, Felix, 118

Brown, John, 56

Browning, Silas W., 25

Brownmiller, Susan, 104, 107–8, 110

Bull, Rice C., 11, 14, 80–81, 140

Bull Run, second battle of, 156

Burns, Anthony, 56

Burnside, Ambrose, 155–56

Bushnell, Horace, 124

Butler, Benjamin F., 103–4, 154

Bye, E. P., 40

Carroll, Henry, 33

Cemeteries, 137, 145–46

Chancellorsville, battle of, 11, 27, 77, 149, 156

Chapin, Leander, 34

Chaplains, 83

Children: blacks as, 57–69; Confederates as, 15–16, 116–17, 132–33; women as, 128–29

Citizenship: and authority, 54; and blacks, 64–65; and discipline, 54; and manhood, 4–18; and soldiering, 4–18, 25, 64–65

Civilians: Civil War as a war against, 100–113; transformation of, into soldiers, 21–22, 35–37

Civil War: blacks blamed for the, 107; casualties of the, 138, 155, 157; as a disciplinary measure, 125–26; disillusionment following the, 137–38; as divine punishment for national sins, 119–20; domesticity as an influence on the outcome of the, 159–66; family/home as a methaphor for the, 37, 116–17, 120; goals of the, 15–16; guilt about the, 69; human cost of the, 157; military technology in the, 155; motivations for fighting, 152–66; results of the, 17, 126; southern women blamed for the, 86, 87, 96, 101; strategy/tactics in the, 155–57; and strengthening of national authority, 121–23, 125–26; as a war against tyranny, 124; as a war of annihilation, 156–57. *See also* War

Clarke, Herman, 121–23, 125

Class issues, 23, 33, 42–43

Cold Harbor, battle of, 157

College athletics, 17

Columbia, S.C., burning of, 89, 107

Community: and a centralized/localized military, 22; company (military unit) as a, 21–23; importance of, 21; influence on sexual relations of, 19–20, 30–31, 35–36; and military authority, 23, 25; and military discipline, 21, 26, 28, 30–31; and officer–soldier relations, 23–24, 25, 28, 30–31; and sacrificing men to war, 25; soldiers' disillusionment with the, 32–35; and the transformation of civilians into soldiers, 21–22, 35–37

Company (military unit), 21–23, 152–53, 158–60

"Comrades, I Am Dying" (song), 142

Condolence letters, 84–86

Confederates: attitudes toward death of, 142; as children, 15–16, 116–17,

65; and the Union occupation, 89, 100–113, 163–65; violence against, 102–10
South Mountain, battle of, 83
Spanish-American War (1898), 17
Stephens, Alexander H., 164
Stevenson, Francis M., 139
Stillwell, Leander, 17, 28, 31, 52, 97, 115
Storrow, Samuel, 144
Strong, Robert, 102
Sutton, Robert, 57
Swearing. *See* Profanity
Swisshelm, Jane, 80

Taylor, Walter H., 162

Ullmann, Daniel, 65
Union. *See* Government/Union
Union occupation, 89, 100–113, 163–65
United States, role in history of, 118–19

Vallandigham affair, 122, 126
Values: community influence on military, 24–25; conflicts between community and military, 35–37. *See also* Morality
Van Alstyne, Lawrence, 146, 158
Vinton, Charley, 39–40
Violence: and self-discipline, 11–12, 105, 106; sexual, 102–10; and soldiering as a rite of passage, 8–10, 11–12; soldiers' become inured to, 32; against women, 102–10
Virtue. *See* Feminine virtue
Volunteerism: and Confederates, 160; effects on outcome of Civil War of, 153–55; and the military as a community, 22–23, 24, 25; and motivation for enlisting, 45–46; and soldiering as a rite of passage, 12–13. *See also* Enlistments/reenlistments

Wainwright, Charles S., 23–24
Walker, Alexander, 103

Walker, William, 67
Walters, Ronald G., 93
War: as ennobling, 147–50; going off to, 5–6; as a maturing process, 4–18; as natural, 17; redemptive nature of, 148, 149; as romance, 17; sacrificing men to, 25; and sex, 111–12. *See also* Civil War; Soldiering; Soldiers
Warrenton, Va., 99
Waterbury, George, 27
Waters, Lucien P., 48
Waters, Ronald G., 108
Weigley, Russell, 156
Wheelock, Julia S., 80, 148
Wheelock, Oliver, 148
Wilderness campaign, 13, 148, 152, 157
Wiley, John S., 45
WIlson, Edmund, 69
Winchester, Va., 99
Woman's Order, 103–4
Women: abandoned, 102–3; as center of domesticity, 72–75; as children, 128–29; as a component of the military, 75–82; and the cult of true womanhood, 92–97; military service as a defense of, 74; and morality, 79, 86; northern women's critique of southern, 93–97; and nurture, 74–75; respect for, 90; sexual anger against, 102–10, 111–12; and soldiering as a rite of passage, 13; soldiers disguised as, 71–72; soldiers' need for, 71–87; as sweethearts/wives, 76–77; violence against, 102–10; and volunteering to go to war, 13. *See also* Feminine virtue; Mothers/maternalism; Nurses/nursing; Sisters/sisterhood; Southern women
Women's benevolent societies, 121
Woodruff, Mathew, 105
World War I, 111–12, 136, 137
Wormeley, Katharine, 78, 147–48
Wren, James, 13, 53, 83